From Rice To Risotto

DAVIDE PAOLINI   MICHELA VUGA

From Rice To Risotto

CARTAGO
LONDON

Published by Cartago
An imprint of KEA Publishing Services Ltd
63 Edith Grove, London SW10 0LB

www.cartago.net
info@cartago.net

Translation
Caroline Phipps

Revised by
Maria Antonia Menini

Art Director
Giorgio Seppi

Editorial Coordination
Mietta Molon

Editorial Direction
Progetto Media, Milano

Project Director
Lella Povia

Editor
Pier Angela Mazzarino

Cover
Studio Priori, Milan

Original Title: Dal Riso ai Risotti
© 1999 Arnoldo Mondadori Editore S.p.A.

Printed in Spain by
Artes Gráficas Toledo, S.A.
D.L. TO: 1125-2000

ISBN 1-900826-29-1

Picture Credits
a: above; c: centre; b: below; l: left; r: right

Agenzia Chimera/Raimondo Santucci, Milan: pp. 99, 106, 107, 114, 115, 118, 119, 120, 121, 122, 123, 132l
Archivio fotografico Electa, Milan: pp. 23, 43ar, 44
Roberto Barisani, Canneto sull'Oglio: p. 103
Franco Bello, Costigliole d'Asti: p. 87
Benito Benevento, Modena: pp. 112, 113
Franco Cantoni, Mortara: p. 85
Centro Documentazione Mondadori, Segrate: pp.14, 31r, 45
Mario Firinaiu, Olbia: pp. 116, 117
Fotografica Foglia, Naples: pp. 126, 127
Foto Leandro/Walter Merlo, Treviso: pp. 108, 109
Foto Phos/Fernando Zanetti, Verona: pp. 93, 128, 129
Valeria Gilardi, Trino Vercellese: p. 101
Maj-Britt Idström, Milan: pp. 3r, 4, 5, 6-7, 8, 12, 13a, 49, 51, 52, 54, 55, 56, 57, 58, 59, 60, 61, 62, 63, 64, 65, 66, 67, 68, 69, 70, 71, 72, 73, 74, 75, 76, 77, 78, 79, 80, 81
Ikona, Rome: p. 25
Itinera Edizioni, Milan: pp. 2r, 21, 22, 27, 30, 31l, 33, 34, 35al, 36ab, 40ar, 41al, 42al
Giorgio Lapris, Crema: p. 95
Guido Mannucci, Florence: pp. 83, 110, 111
Massimo Mazzilli, Milan: pp. 2l, 13c and b, 15, 16-17, 18,19, 20, 24, 26, 28-29, 32, 35c and bl, 36r and c, 37, 38, 39, 40ab and c, 41br, 42ar, 43ab and cl, 46, 47, 47, 130, 131, 132r, 133, 134, 135, 136, 137
Ortolan/Bison, Mogliano Veneto: p. 91
Mauro Raffini, Turin: p. 105
Service Photo Color/Davide Bellani, Parma: p. 97
Mark Edward Smith, Venice: pp. 124, 125
Studio 57/Renato Garanzini, Stradella: p. 89
Studio L'Atelier, Modena: pp. 82, 84, 86, 88, 90, 92, 94, 96, 98, 100, 102, 104

Contents

Introduction

Risotto is not a trade mark like *Made in Italy*, but it could well be, because all risottos speak the same language, albeit in many dialects, in fact as many as towns, provinces and regions there are in Italy...

In every corner of the country you will find a restaurant or a trattoria that cooks rice according to the local tradition and with the ingredients of the land, a happy combination established way back in the past due to the lack of communications and limited exchanges. And even where no specific tradition prevails, there is always a creative and resourceful cook familiar with the frying technique, the amount of fats to add, the stock making, the cooking times, the correct varieties of rice... and the wisdom to know when to use the wooden spoon and the copper ladle... in short, a universal language throughout the world of rice cooking.

Rice, a versatile companion

Rice is an adaptable product allowing innumerable combinations: meat, fish, vegetables, wines, truffles, mushrooms. In rice-growing Lombardy alone, (whose capital, Milan, is said to be the birthplace of the first risotto to go down in history, saffron rice or risotto *alla milanese*) traditional rice dishes include river fish (crabs), lake fish (pike, tench, perch), pumpkin, paprika, nettles, hop shoots, borlotti beans and goose sausage, pork sausages and chops, local sausage (Brinza), frogs (Pavia), among others. The same occurs in the provinces of Vercelli and Novara and in the rest of Piedmont, where wine, truffles and all types of sausages are among the most usual companions of a rice dish. We could say the same of the Veneto, where all types of vegetables play a leading role in rice dishes.

Multiform risotto

Some say risotto is an exclusively Paduan dish. It certainly is true that the land crossed by the longest river in the country, the Po, is a leader rice-growing area where the best cooking varieties (Carnaroli, Vialone nano, Arborio, Baldo, Roma) are produced. But over time, this extraordinary first course (and in some cases, main dish) has spread and been absorbed by local gastronomic cultures throughout the country. One only needs to take a look at the different ways seafood rice is presented from the Adriatic to the Tyrrhenian Seas, not to mention the Islands. And there are other important traditional rice dishes, such as the *tiella* in the Puglia, the *pilau* in Sardinia and the *sartù* in Naples. For rice fundamentalists these dishes, together with timbales and Venetian *minestre fisse* (*risi e bisi*, rice and green peas,) cannot be counted as rice dishes, but on no account can they be ignored.

Another radical school of opinion classifies rice-based dishes according to the cutlery used to eat them: if a spoon is required then it is a *menester*. Actually, good table manners dictate that risotto is eaten with a folk, which confirms that it should not be too liquid, but rather compact, with the grains blended but not sticking together.

Whatever the case, in Italy rice is an object of absolute cult, with its own firmly defended local cooking techniques which, in the case of the risotto all produce a deliciously creamy and crunchy rice dish.

In addition to the wide disparity in cooking methods, the paternity of certain rice dishes is also subject to dispute. For example, the invention of the rice bomb is generally credited to Parma, but some extend its origin to Piacenza and yet others who are convinced that the dish comes from Lunigiana and is, therefore, Tuscan. Pellegrino Artusi, author of *La scienza in cucina e l'arte di mangiar bene*, a relevant text written at the end of the nineteenth century, was one of the few authors who did his best to offer an overall view of Italian recipes. Pellegrino credits Florence with the invention of black rice with cuttlefish, and while the use of beets in the recipe distinguishes the Florentine from the Venetian version, Venice is being generally accepted as the origin of this dish. And what about the elaborate Neapolitan *sartù* (from the French *surtout*, meaning "above all"). Is it accurate to classify it as a timbale when it contains a rich and varied stuffing under a risotto covering? Just how many different historical, technical, lexical and gastronomic interpretations can this extremely widespread and popular dish generate?

Rice plays a leading role in cooking recipes throughout the world - an extremely versatile product that lends itself to endless delicious combinations.

The risotto culture

To put it briefly, the preparation of a risotto demands a completely Italian "culture". It is absurd to sell dishes like vodka rice with orange, rice with pears and red wine or rice with strawberries, ham and melon as Italian. These dishes are good examples of refrigerator patchwork, the fantasy of someone out of ideas and with no time to spare; or of someone who had the misfortune to enter a pseudotrattoria with rather muddled ideas on *nouvelle cuisine*.

Fruit, starting with strawberries and kiwis, are not ingredients of a genuine Italian risotto and recipes that include them, pompously called "creative risottos", may only be justified in Hawaii or in the tropics. The only outstanding risotto in Italian cuisine that includes fruit as an ingredient is one created by Pina Bellini, long-standing chef at the Scaletta, one of the most extraordinary restaurants that has ever existed in Milan. This risotto is made with myrtle berries and pork. But the Oscar for originality goes to the Milanese chef Gualtiero

Marchesi, who surprised everybody a few years ago by putting a gold leaf on saffron rice.

Risotto is unquestionably "marked" by the DOC of Italian cooking. Auguste Escoffier, the great master of classical cuisine, clears any doubt on the question by always adding "Italian-style" when talking of risotto in his *Guida alla grande cucina*. He also describes Florentine, Milanese, Piedmontese and vigil rice. So the adjective "Italian" coming from a real authority on the matter confirms the cultural, linguistic and culinary identity of risotto, as well as its historical origins, without requiring further confirmation. But if this were needed, one would only have to read the memorable passage, in a personal and somewhat archaistic style, by Carlo Emilio Gadda, in his *Meraviglie d'Italia*:

> *Hold the pot on the heat by the handle with the left hand protected with a felt oven glove. Add slices or tiny pieces of tender onion, and a quarter ladleful of broth, preferably broth that is on the heat and made with veal; add top-quality Lodi butter. The amount of butter, quantum prodest, taking into account the number of people at table. When this reasonable portion of butter and the onion start to fry gently, add small quantities of rice until reaching a total of two or three handfuls per person, depending on their expected appetite. The little broth added is not enough for the rice to start the boiling process; this is where the spoon (wooden) really plays its role: stir and stir again. In the next phase of the ritual, the grains become brown and firm in contact with the hot, burning, bottom, each one keeping its own "personality": neither sticking together nor going lumpy.*
>
> *Quantum sufficit butter, never again, please; it must not form a sauce, or a stocky stew: it must oil each grain, not drown it. The rice must go firm, as we said, on the hot bottom. Then it gradually swells, and cooks, by the gradual addition of the broth, with which you must be cautious, and accurate: add each time a little broth, starting with two half-ladleful which you have ready at hand in a bowl in which you have previously dissolved the powder saffron - a vivacious, unequalled stimulant of the gastric system - produced by the stigmas, duly dried and ground, of the saffron*

Threshing season in the
ricefields that flank the
access to a farmstead in
Candia (Lomellina).

flower. For eight people, dissolve two small coffee spoonfuls. With the addition of the saffron the broth takes on a colour between yellow and mandarin, and the risotto, at its optimum cooking point, twenty or twenty-two minutes later, will be orange-yellow. For timid stomachs two levels and not heaped coffee spoonfuls will be sufficient: in this case the rice will be a canary yellow colour. The most important thing during the whole ritual is to maintain a god-fearing spirit, full of respect for the reverend Aesculapius and only use first-quality ingredients in the sacred "risotto alla milanese": the aforesaid Vialone with the aforesaid veste lacera and the aforesaid little slices of tender onion; for the broth, a veal cooked with carrots and celery, all three from the Padana plain, and not a retired bull, of Balcanic temperament and horns. In respect to saffron, Carlo Erba Milano advised sealed packets which would mean ten or twelve, maximum fifteen, liras per person. Half a cigarette! Do not deceive the gods, do not forget Aesculapius, do not betray your family or your guests, protected by Jupiter, by denying the Carlo Erba Company their gains. No! And on the butter, in absence of Lodi's, you can confidently replace it with butter from Melegnano, Casalbuttano Soresina, Melzo or Casalpusterlengo, or from anywhere in the southern Milanese region below the risorgive area from Ticino to Adda and to Crema and Cremona. To margarine I say no! And no also to butter tasting of soap!

Among possible additions -even recommended or demanded by the superexperts on the subject - are marrow (beef), unjustly ignored and delicately reserved to other uses in marginal dishes. These are usually added to the rice, at least one per guest, more or less halfway through cooking and the duty of a good risotto cook is to stir and blend them with the spoon (wooden, of course. Marrow gives risotto, in the same degree as the carefully measured butter, a sober creaminess, as well as favouring, apparently, the haematopoietic function of our own bone marrow. Two or more spoonfuls of full-bodied (Piedmont) red wine, without being compulsory, will give the dish, for those who like it, an aromatic flavour that accelerates and favours digestion. The risotto alla milanese must not be overcooked...no! That never! Just the slightest bit more than al dente: the grain dissolved and swollen with each one of the juices but still individual, not stuck to its companions, not forming a mass swimming in a broth which would be unpleasant. Risotto experts hardly admit Parmesan; it is a combination of Milanese sobriety and elegance. When the first September rains fall, fresh mushrooms will end up in the pans; and after Saint Martin's day, dry truffle flakes cut with a special instrument in the shape of a clover leaf may be spread on the risotto. And neither mushrooms nor truffles manage to distort the deep, vital and noble meaning of the risotto alla milanese.

[1960]

Carlo Emilio Gadda
Le meraviglie d'Italia
Einaudi, Turín 1964

Rice:

Past and Present

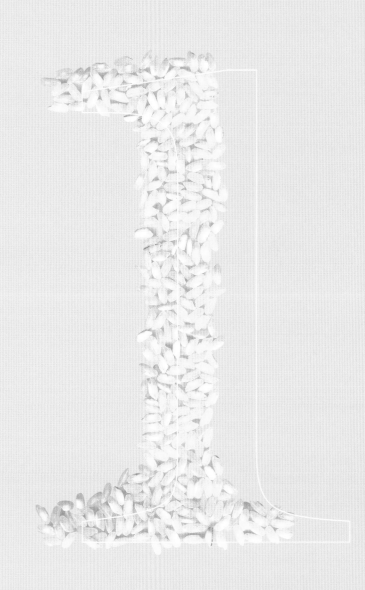

Rice: past and present

Rice (*Oryza*) is an annual plant of the Gramineae family. After corn, it is the most widespread cereal on earth and the staple diet of more than one-half of the world population. Over the centuries it has given origin to two cultivated species: the predominating *Oryza sativa* of Asian origin, and *Oryza glaberrima* of African origin, whose production is currently decreasing.

Oryza sativa has gradually branched out into three subspecies: *indica*, grown in India, from which varieties such as Basmati, Long Thai and Long Grain have derived; *javanica*, grown mainly in Indonesia; and *japonica*, from which all the Italian varieties derive by hybridization.

It is interesting to note that while rice is one of the oldest and most consumed food products, it comprises ultramodern features: it is global, being grown in most areas of the world; multinational, present on the shelves of practically all stores on the planet; and multiethnic, appearing in a wide range of recipes throughout the world.

A past surrounded in mystery

Given its universal features, it is surprising how little is really known about the history of rice, starting with the origin of its name, *orysa*, from which the current scientific term *oryza*, proceeds.

Some scholars uphold the theory that it stems from the word *arisi*, the ancient Tamil term for rice. Others point to the ancient city of Orissa on the east coast of India, a marshy area in the Gulf of Bengal, as one

of the main rice growing, harvesting and exporting centres, but do not specify whether the word *orysa* gave its name to the city or vice versa.

Not only is the origin of the word obscure, but also the graminea itself. Some experts believe that rice is not a spontaneous grass, but the product of a natural selection.

Others think that it started growing on the isle of Java or in Cambodia, and according to yet another theory it first appeared in Northeast China from where it spread to Japan, Indonesia, India and Syria. Whatever the case, archaeologists have found bowls containing grains of rice in settlements located along the river Mekong dating back to 6000 BC.

Rice comes West

Here too, it is not clear how exactly rice (understood as a product of mass consumption) found its way to the West. It appears that rice was unknown in Egypt or in Palestine before the birth of Christ, as neither historical Egyptian or biblical sources mention it.

In Greece and Rome

Rice could well have been brought to Greece from the East by Alexander the Great's soldiers.

The Romans knew about rice, but considered it a spice and had it imported from the East by their merchants. As with all rare and dear eastern spices and drugs, it was sold at an extremely high price, a luxury only the privileged could afford. Even then it was only used as a medicine in infusions and decoctions, and also to

Scenes of daily life in a Roman fresco. In ancient Rome rice was a rare and dear product, imported from the East as a spice. Wealthy women used in to prepare beauty products.

Left: Different types of rice: (top to bottom) brown, parboiled, Basmati and fine.

thicken sauces. Wealthy women applied it in pomade form to obtain softer and more luminous skin. It appears also that gladiators and athletes drank a rice-based decoction as stimulant: *"doping" ante litteram*.

In the Middle Ages

Little is know on the use and growth of rice in the Middle Ages. There are different opinions on the subject and reliable records are scarce. One theory is that in the eighth century rice-growing was introduced by the Arabs into Spain from where it passed on to Sicily; another that it was the Crusades who made it known in northern Italy.

However, Pier de'Crescenzi, the famous fourteenth century writer on agriculture who catalogued 293 vegetable species and 350 plants, does not mention rice even once.

Others assert that rice was grown for the first time, to be used as medicine (a vegetal or "simple" remedy, as medicinal plants were then called), in the eleventh century in the vegetable gardens of the convents of the Neapolitan region as a result of the widespread fame acquired by the medical theories of the celebrated school of Salerno. The rice consumed in

Rice growing spread to Italy at the end of the Middle Ages, probably introduced into Europe by the Arabs.

Christmas sweetmeats.

The presence of grains in Lombardy (but not their cultivation) is officially documented in a bylaw of 1336 issued by the Tax Court of Milan, by which apothecaries could not sell it at more than 12 imperials to the pound, while the price of honey was established at 8 imperials. The statute does not specify the origin of this product, referring to it simply as an imported spice.

Ricefields in Italy

The first reliable document offering unobjectionable proof that rice was grown in Italy, and more specifically in Lombardy, is a letter dated the 27th September 1475 in which Galeazzo Maria Sforza, Duke of Milan, undertakes to deliver to the ambassador of the Duke of Ferrara twelve sacks of rice to be sown in the Ferrara region, an area appropriate for growing this cereal. In 1494, Giangaleazzo Sforza enacted a bylaw forbidding the sale of both the product and the seeds outside his dukedom; but the edict did not produce the expected effect.

During this period rice growing was spreading to different areas of Italy, starting in Piedmont and the Veneto. In the Verona region in particular, several wealthy landowners promoted the development of the new grain taking advantage of the hydric potential in the area south of Verona, between the rivers Po and Adige. Between 1558 and 1604 an estimate of 1 448 ha were dedicated to rice fields, and by the middle of the sixteenth century there were over 5 500 hectares of ricefields in the Milanese region.

In spite of the above, it is worth mentioning that rice northern Italy, however, was imported from the East. This was a profitmaking trade, prerogative of the Venetian merchants; indeed, in spite of the favourable environmental conditions, the Serenissima obstructed its cultivation in order to speculate with customs duties and import taxes.

Around 1250 the term "riso" appeared in the records of the hospital Sant'Andrea of Vercelli, and account books of the House of Savoy mention the purchase of several hectograms of rice to be used in specific

LA
COLTIVAZIONE
DEL RISO
DEL MARCHESE
GIAN BATTISTA SPOLVERINI
AL CATTOLICO RE
FILIPPO QUINTO.

IN VERONA,
CIƆIƆCCLVIII.
Per Agostino Carattoni Stampator del Seminario Vescovile.
Con Licenza de' Superiori.

Fran: Lorenzi dis.

Cunego inc. Ver.

DELLA
COLTIVAZIONE
DEL RISO
LIBRO III.

23

Old sickles and rice sheaves decorating the walls of the Cascina Gattinera di Ferrera Erbognone (Pavia).

Below: Trademark of an old hulling machine, restored and used in the Cascina Gattinera for preparing rice. The traditional method preserves the natural qualities of the product.

was not yet included in its own right in Italian cuisine. Rice started being considered proper food even for those with no particular health problem thanks, specifically, to the work of the Sienese physician Pier Andrea Mattioti (1500-1577. In his *I Discorsi di Messer Pietro Andrea Mattioli, medico cesareo, sui sei libri di Dioscoride Pedanio Anazarbos della materia medicale*, ("Lectures of master Pietro Andrea Mattioli, from Siena, caesarian physician, on six books by Dioscoride Pedanio Anazarbos on medical subjects"), published in Venice in 1544. Mattioli included a eulogy of rice, which he defined as very digestible, tasty and fortifying.

Rice-growing continued spreading in Lombardy and by the eighteenth century covered 20,000 hectares, but over the following hundred years it suffered a drastic reduction in favour of pastures. In the Piedmont, on the other hand, the development of rice was slower due to the lack of irrigation channels. Official French cadastral documents show that around 1800 42,000 ha of rice was planted in the area between Santhià, Biella and Vercelli, and that in 1860 in the Vercelli area alone the figure reached 30,000 hectares. But Italian rice growing really bloomed with the opening of the Cavour canal, built between 1866 and 1874, covering an extension of 232,000 hectares, with 145,000 in Lombardy alone (these figures should not be interpreted literally; at that time statistics were not an exact science). Lombardy, Piedmont and Veneto were not the only regions with bylaws, edicts and decrees that confirm the reality of rice growing between the end of the sixteenth century and the first half of the nineteenth century. Clear signs of rice crops are also to be found in Romagna and in the regions of Ravenna and Bologna (over 9 000 hectares in 1880).

The crisis

The opening of the Suez canal in 1869 dealt an almost fatal blow to Italian production, as the Asian varieties of rice turned out to be serious competitors, so much so that the Italian Government, pressured by the farmers' lobbies, was forced to pass a law (30th June 1890) in order to increase import duties on rice and also to establish a series of surcharges to check imports of competing products into Italy. The approximately 230,000 hectares of rice crops recorded during the four-year 1870-1874 period fell to 164,000 in 1893.

But neither tariff barriers nor protectionist policies solved the problems in the sector, which lasted until World War I, when the tendency reversed, i.e. an increase in both internal demand and in prices took place.

But the problems reappeared after the war, with

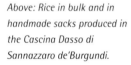

Asian competition as fierce as ever. Some authors maintain that the decrease in internal consumption was due to the rejection on the part of war veterans who had been forced to eat a kind of tepid and repulsive rice-based porridge during months on end in the trenches.

The blackest period occurred between 1929 and 1933, the time of the Wall Street disaster and of the world economic crisis, which had serious consequences in Italy as well.

In 1931 the National Rice Department (Ente Nazionale Risi) was founded, with the object of defending Italian production through premiums to exports, bills of sale with foreign governments and the building of depots and drying plants for collective use. Among other things, the Ente Risi launched one of the first large-scale promotional campaigns in favour of an agrofood product.

When World War II broke out, the situation of rice crops in Italy fell drastically again: the 900,000 tons harvested in 1941 decreased to 300,000 in 1945, while the cultivated area dropped from 167,000 to

96,000 hectares.

After the war activity recovered slowly due, among other things, to the Korean conflict of 1952, when rice exports from that country to Europe decreased. Thus, with ups and downs, rice makes its way to the European Community.

Rice today

Today, with a surface area of 215,000 hectares, Italy is the first rice-producing country in Europe. The average annual output per hectare is 5500-6000 kilos of rice (2300-2400 kilos in the nineteenth century)

and total annual output over 1300 million kilos. Quantitatively, production remains stable in the 7000 farms and 40 industrial estates due to Asian and American competition in respect to long-grain (only in the B category with Thaibonnet leading) and parboiled (this rice is treated to boil rapidly without overcooking) varieties.

Italy has never been competitive in these qualities of rice, used mostly as garnish. On the other hand it has been, and definitely still is, unique and unbeatable in top-qualities rice used in main courses, especially risottos. (Carnaroli, Vialone nano, Arborio, Baldo, Roma, San'Andrea and Balilla are among these varieties).

In haute cuisine rice dishes, Italy is the unquestionable leader, but the consumption of rice is still low, being used mainly in recipes that require careful preparation and a high gastronomic know-how.

The main Italian rice-growing areas are located in the provinces of Vercelli, Novara, Alessandria, Biella, Pavia, Milan, Lodi, Verona, Rovigo, Ferrara, Mantua, Modena, Reggio Emilia, Ancona, Cosenza, Oristano and Cagliari.

Above: Ripe ears of rice bent under the weight of the grains. Just one plant can produce up to a hundred grains.

The map below shows the main rice producer countries in the world; as can be seen, rice crops spread over all the continents.

Rice in Italy:

From Paddy to Pot

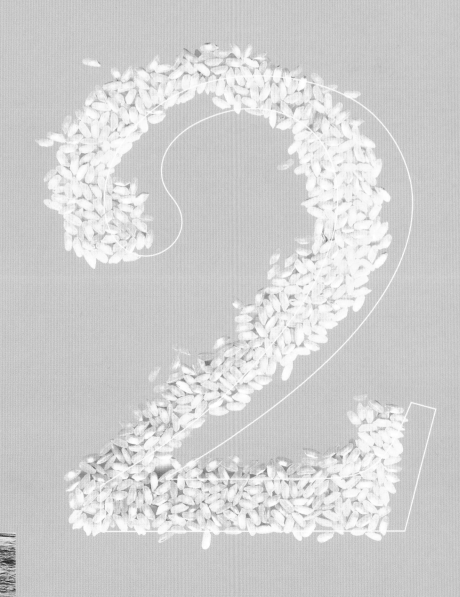

Rice in Italy: from paddy to pot

There appear to be over fifty varieties of rice grown in Italy, but their classification is hampered by the fact that each year some disappear or are produced in insufficient quantities, such as Razza 77 (predecessor of Baldo), Maratelli or Giant Vercelli.

On the other hand, there are several traditional easily located production areas: the Pavia region to the area of Vercelli-Novara and the Verona region. Although rice is grown in other parts of Italy, these regions yield almost 90 percent of total Italian output.

Lombardy

This region coincides with the Padana Plain, situated between the river Po (closely associated to the development of rice in Italy) and the lower course of the Ticino and the Sesia, and contains a dense network of canals and large imposing brick farmsteads. In springtime the landscape becomes one great iridescent lake - this is the miracle of rice, which changes the colours and the textures of the land.

Pavia, where rice has been grown since the times of Ludovic the Moor, is unquestionably the leading productive area of Lombardy, with 85,000 hectares of ricefields. These farms not only produce the largest amount of Italian rice, but also the highest proportion of the three best quality varieties, the choice of great chefs, gourmets and experts, namely, Arborio (45 percent of national production), Vialone nano (43 percent) and in particular Carnaroli (60 percent). All three varieties are particularly appropriate for preparing risotti, so it is not by chance that the Pavia region is the birthplace of this famous dish, in which other traditional produce of the land such as frogs, sausages, vegetables and fresh water fish are also used.

Apart from the unquestionable leadership of Pavia, there are other top-quality Lombardy ricefields in the adjacent Milan area and also in the province of Mantua, two regions proud of their own tradition in risotti.

Piedmont

Piedmont, with the provinces of Vercelli and Novara in the lead, has the largest extension of ricefields (117,000 hectares) and cultivates different varieties of rice, including the extrafine categories such as Arborio, Volano and Roma, as well as a limited production of Carnaroli and Baldo. In addition to the provinces of Vercelli (67,000 ha) and Novara (33,000 ha), there are also ricefields in Biella and Alessandria. As well as growing the best qualities for risotto, Piedmont producers have lately made efforts to compete with the Americans and the East by cultivating varieties most in demand in the international market (among them, the Thaibonnet). The Piedmont region has a strong rice tradition and

The map of Italy labels the following regions: TRENTINO, FRIULI, LOMBARDY, VENETO, PIEMONTE, EMILIA ROMAGNA, TUSCANY, MARCHE, UMBRIA, ABRUZZO, LAZIO, MOLISE, CAMPANIA, PUGLIA, BASILICATA, CALABRIA, SARDINIA, SICILY

Growing rice plantlets. At this stage the ricefields change colour, and grass green dominates the scenery.

Right: Grains of different types of rice.

Left: Map of Italy showing the main rice-growing areas. There are over fifty varieties of Italian rice.

here the risotto al dente reigns, always accompanied by local wines, in particular Barbera, a red wine used frequently in recipes. As the proverb goes: "Rice is born in water and dies in wine".

Like a flower in their buttonhole, each region or even each province has its typical dish: *panissa* in the Vercelli region, *paniscia* around Novara, *ris an cagnon* in the Biella area.

Veneto

The Veronese Bassa, where local rice has been consumed since the sixteenth century, forms the third side of the triangle of top-quality rice. Here the main variety is Vialone nano, a semifine rice introduced as far back as 1937. The area is abundant in large rivers and has its own particular climate, both factors essential for the production of aprox. 9,000,000 kilos of rice on almost 2000 hectares of land and thirty-three farms, assembled in a Consortium for the specific protection of the Vialone nano.

In the Verona region the rice is sown between the end of April and the first fortnight in May. The growing cycle lasts about 155 days. During the draining stage, the carps that the farmers had placed in the ricefields to eliminate insects and weeds are fished out again. To protect the Veronese Vialone nano, a Consortium was founded as early as 1977, with the object of ensuring respect and maintenance of the environment on the part of the rice farmers and industries. For this, in 1996 the EU commission granted the Veronese Vialone nano the IGP

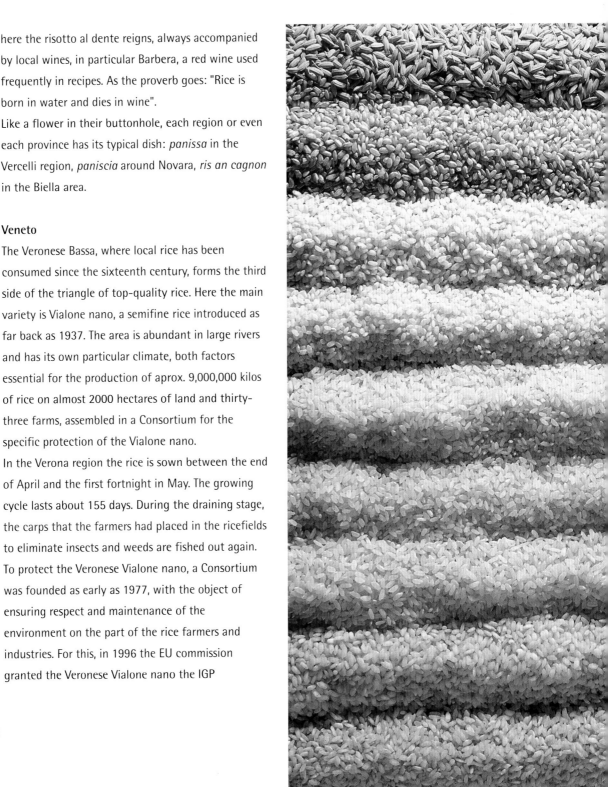

Ricefields in the Pavia region during threshing time. In the centre, an irrigation channel. The availability of water is essential in rice growing, although currently efforts have been made to dry-grow it.

distinction (Protected Geographical Indication), a unique case in Europe in the sector. The farms and industries' members of the Association undertook not to use chemicals and to eliminate parasites and weeds by natural means, such as the use of carps in the ricefields mentioned above, and a technique designed to eliminate naturally a specific weed, the *giavone* from the ricefields. This method consists in maintaining the level of water in the ricefields at a height such that allows the rice to grow but completely covers the *giavone* which dies in a short time from lack of air.

Other Italian ricefield regions

Apart from Lombardy, Piedmont and Veneto (where only the ricefields in the province of Rovigo cover an extension greater to those of the Verona region), the grain is also cultivated in Emilia (about 10,000 ha), Tuscany (500 ha), Calabria (400 ha) and Sardinia (400 ha).

A newcomer to the sector is the Marche region, where in the past rice-growing had been abandoned in favour of corn in compliance with a royal law of 1866 that imposed the rotation of crops. Rice has

been planted experimentally here since 1994, the novelty being the "dry production" method, that is, using a quantity of water similar to that required for producing corn.

The Consortium was created in order to protect, (although perhaps even more to promote) certain varieties of Italian rice that have unique organoleptic properties. It is a free-membership association of producers (rice farms), transformers (rice industries) and producers-transformers of several regions, with the purpose of establishing a quality control policy for the most appreciated varieties (Balilla, Baldo, Carnaroli, Sant'Andrea and Vialone nano). The varieties of rice protected by the Consortium cover approximately 50,000 ha (about 26 percent of the national total).

Cultivation

In the case of Italy, the most strenuous operation in the rice-growing cycle was at one time carried out by thousands of workers, most of whom were women. From the 50's onwards these tasks became gradually easier with the use of selective fertilisers and products for eliminating weeds, and today they are

completely mechanised.

Rice-growing consists of four main phases: preparing the terrain, flooding the plots and sowing, eliminating weeds and harvesting.

Preparing the land

The preparation of the ricefields starts in spring: the fields are ploughed to silt the large clods of fresh earth that were resting under the surface crust during winter. The land is then levelled and fertilised. In recent years, an increasing number of machines equipped with electronic apparatus and laser rays are

used to improve the levelling of the surface.

Flooding and sowing

The plots are then flooded and the ricefields become artificial lagoons. The water is obtained directly from the rivers or the thick network of irrigation canals. A layer of water of about ten centimetres is essential for the development of the seedlings, whose vegetative cycle varies from 150 and 180 days; among other things, it protects the germinating seeds and then the seedlings from thermal night/day variations.

From three to ten thousand litres of water are required to obtain one kilo of rice. The level of the water must be controlled during the entire cycle. Sowing is done in April, an annual task carried out in all the areas. The mechanical sewers are pulled by tractors equipped with special cogged iron wheels for smooth progress in the mud.

Weeding

In June the ricefields are cleared of all plants that subtract nourishment from the rice; this operation (traditionally done by women workers) is currently carried out with the help of specific weeding products.

Harvesting

One of the most evocative moments of the rice-growing cycle is harvesting time, from the beginning of September to mid-October. The harvesters

On this page, weeding and rice harvesting. Before agriculture was mechanised, these strenuous operations were carried out by hand in Italy (as they still are in the East) and the workers were familiar figures in the ricefields landscapes.

accomplish a very large amount of work in a very short time; right there in the field they rapidly cut the rice and separate it from the straw.

Transformation

Before being commercialised the rice undergoes several different transformation processes which generate products that are progressively either more refined or acquire specific features.

Drying

The freshly harvested rough, or paddy, rice has a humidity of between 20 and 30 percent. It is therefore transported to drying plants to lose approximately half its humidity and to ensure it suffers no deterioration before being milled. By law, the humidity index of rice sold on the market cannot exceed 15 percent..

Hulling

The transformation of rough to edible rice can be briefly divided into two main phases. The first is known as hulling and consists in removing the outer hull, or husk, by friction. The product obtained is edible brown rice, the kernel still surrounded by bran layers rich in fast-modifying fats that hinder their conservation (which is why these varieties are for short-term consumption or vacuum preserved).

Whiting

The second milling process removes by abrasion the bran layers of the kernel to obtain commercial white rice. The first whiting operation produces semi-elaborated rice.

Semi-refined and refined rice are produced, respectively, after two more refining operations and an ultimate separation of the whole grains from the broken ones.

Polishing and glossing

For aesthetic reasons the rice may undergo further processes: polishing (the grains are smoothed and treated with Vaseline oil, obtaining the *camolino* rice) and given a glossy finish (the grains are rubbed with a chemical solution of glucose and talc obtaining glazed rice).

Sowing starts in April in the flooded ricefields; in Italy this operation is carried out by centrifugal sowers, which scatter the seeds regularly in the water.

The rice is ripe and ready to be reaped with the ears now a golden colour.
Far right: Harvest time.

its almost complete lack of cellulose. It is very nutritive (with a higher energetic value than any other cereal) because of the particular nature of its starch, which is immediately absorbed by the organism.

To get an idea of the output of the milling processes, which in turn may throw light on sales prices, one hundred kilos of rough rice are required to produce sixty kilos of refined rice.

Above these lines: ricefields after threshing.

Output

During the refining process, the grain loses many of its nutrients, which are largely contained in its outer layers or bran (rich in proteins, fats and mineral salts) and in the husk (eliminated during the hulling process and subsequently used as livestock feed). More refined is the rice, more numerous are the nutrients that have been eliminated.

But at the same time, the milling processes undergone by the rice are necessary to make it edible. And of course even refined and glazed rice is still a complete, healthy and nutritious food. As in the case of pastas, rice is made up mainly of carbohydrates, with the advantage of being more digestible due to

Parboiling and vitaminizing

In order to recover the nutrients (vitamins and mineral salts in particular) in the outer layers of the grain that were eliminated during the milling, the rice is put through certain technological processes, such as parboiling and vitaminizing.

In the parboiling technique, the rough rice is split, submerged in hot water for the hulling (when the bran is eliminated many of the substances contained in the outer layers of the grains pass into the water). Then the grains are pressure-cooked in the same water in which they were softened; the internal structure of the kernel changes (the starch becomes gelatinous) and almost completely reabsorbs the

Ensilage of the rice (far left) and a dryer (left). When harvested, the rice contains between 20 and 30 per cent of its weight in water. In the past, after the threshing it was spread out on the ground to dry. This operation is currently carried out in the drying plants.

Right: Two views of a granary where the rice is stored before being sold to the refining industries.

mineral salts, proteins and vitamins. The treated rice is then dried until the correct degree of humidity is reached.

The parboiled rice thus obtained is translucent, of an amber or yellowish colour and contains more vitamins and mineral salts than white rice. It is also more consistent and compact, and as a result "behaves" better in cooking, during which it loses less nutrients and absorbs less of the water and fats contained in the added condiments. For all these reasons, it is more nutritious and easier to digest.

The vitaminized variety is produced by mixing grains soaked in a vitamin substance to refined rice, in an approximate ratio of one vitaminized grain to two hundred white grains.

Classification

The classification of rice can vary (sometimes even widely) according to the country. In the rice trade, two parameters are generally used: the size of the grain and legally approved tolerance limits.

But in the past rice was classified according to its use. Originario rice (the name was introduced to distinguish pure Japanese varieties from the local ones; all current Originario varieties derive from the original Omahi or Chinese rice) was considered common rice not because it had a short round grain, but because it was destined to daily use.

In international trade, the distinction is made above all in function of the length of the grain and of its length/width ratio. Its organoleptic properties, its behaviour during cooking or nutritive value are not taken into account at all. This is the reason why grains with a length up to and including 5.2 mm and a length/width ratio below 2 are known as round or short-grain rice. Medium-grain rice measures from 5.2 mm to 6 mm, with a length/width ratio under 3. Finally, long-grain rice is over 6 mm long, with a length/width ratio above 2 and below 3 in type A and equal or above 3 in type B.

Italian nomenclature

Italian law recognises four classes of rice: Common, Semifine, Fine and Superfine. Italian classification also ignores organoleptic properties, nutritive values or resistance in cooking, and refers almost exclusively to the length of the grain. The Superfine category is possibly the one exception, because the authorised varieties in this class have higher organoleptic properties.

Italian law also establishes that all rice on sale indicates on the packet its group and variety. Rice with grains shorter than 5.2 mm are classified as Common (Balilla, Elio, Selenio), between 5.2 and 6.2 mm are Semifine (Argo, Cripto, Lido, Padano, Vialone nano), and longer than 6.2 mm are Fine (Europa, Loto, Riva, Ariete, Cervo, Drago, Ribe, Sant'Andrea). Superfine varieties (Arborio, Baldo, Carnaroli, Roma, Volano) stand out for the length of their grain (long-grain) and their higher organoleptic properties.

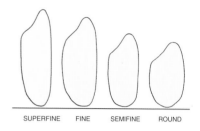

SUPERFINE   FINE   SEMIFINE   ROUND

Above these lines: Naturally-produced rice.

Above right: Rice is classified mainly according to the morphology of the grain.

All these varieties are of the *japonica* subspecies and are excellent for preparing typical Italian dishes because of their creamy consistency due to starch release.

Other types of rice

Many other varieties of the *indica* subspecies can currently be found in the market - their grains are long, transparent, firm and in some cases perfumed. These rices are produced in India, Indonesia,

Bangladesh, Thailand, Japan, Burma, Pakistan, Brazil and the United States, and the grains remain well separated even after lengthy cooking, which is why they are usually used in salads, cold dishes and as garnish in the producer countries and in the north of Europe.

Most of these popular varieties are parboiled, that is,

Classification of the main varieties of Italian rice

GROUP*	VARIETY
Common	
Round Grain	Balilla, Elio, Selenio
Semifine	
Medium	Argo, Cripto, Lido, Padano, Vialone enano
Fine	
Medium	Europa, Loto, Riva
Long A	Ariete, Cervo, Drago, Ribe, Sant'Andrea
Superfine	
Long A	Arborio, Baldo, Carnaroli, Roma, Volano
Long B	Graldo, Panda, Pegaso, Thaibonnet

*Names in italics refer to EU denominations

rice whose grains have undergone a process currently practised on an industrial scale but traditionally applied in India, Pakistan and Burma and which was introduced into Italy, the United States and England in the 1940's. In the steam-pressure parboiling

technique (also applied to special processing of semi-rough rice), the vitamins pass intact from the outer to the inner part of the grain.

This procedure (widely used in the American army during World War II to guarantee the condition of the rice given to the soldiers) gelatinises and stabilises the starch in the grain, thereby offering faster and more predictable cooking. As it does not overcook, parboiled rice is used for pre-prepared dishes that can be kept in the freezer.

One of the most popular non Italian varieties of parboiled rice is Basmati, grown in the north of India and in Pakistan. Its grain is spindle-shaped, translucent and lengthens during cooking. Basmati remains consistent at all times and is appropriate for steam cooking. It has a slight perfume of sandalwood and is classified as aromatic rice. Grown in India, Thailand and Madagascar, this rice has a more or less intense aroma after being steam-cooked; the aroma intensifies after long storage periods as a result of a chemical transformation, of the fat components in particular.

Another popular parboiled variety is the American Patna, grown in California. Its grains remain whole and firm after cooking.

Another variety is the wild or brown rice of the Chippewa Indians of Minnesota that grows in the east of the United States, in the Congo and in north-east Asia. It is not exactly a rice, but a *zizania acquatica* of the Gramineae family. Its caryopsis may measure up to a centimetre long and is of a darker colour.

Above: Grains of rice at different stages of processing.

Right: Baldo, Carnaroli and Thaibonnet varieties, produced at the Cascina Gattinera di Ferrera Erbognone (Pavia).

All varieties of parboiled and fast-cooking rice (parboiled then pre-cooked and dehydrated) are recommended even for pilaff.

From rice to risotto

Among the vast number of varieties available in the Italian and the international market, it may seem difficult to know which rice to chose for the best risotto. But in fact the range of possibilities is fairly limited. What a risotto needs is a rice that absorbs the flavours and produces a deliciously creamy dish.

The five top Italian varieties for this are without doubt Carnaroli, Arborio, Baldo and Vialone nano, to which some chefs add Sant'Andrea and Roma for "regional" or "territorial" rice dishes.

Carnaroli

Both risotto chefs and risotto enthusiasts consider Carnaroli "the king of rices": the centre of the grain is always al dente but it remains creamy when butter and Parmesan cheese are added at the end of the cooking thanks to its starch content. This variety dates back to 1945 and is the result of crossbreeding between Vialone and Lencino. Carnaroli was saved from extinction by a farmer in the Lomellina region in the mid-80's since when it has become increasingly popular.

▪ Features

Appearance: superfine rice; the firm fat elongated grain with spindle-shaped section measures approximately 7 mm.

Colour: cerulean, with small white central pearl and crystalline outer part.

Cooking: cooks in approximately 15 minutes; long-lasting al dente consistency.

Taste: clean, tending to sweet, with firm elastic grains even after cooking.

Use: traditional mountain and sea risottos, with separate and not excessively creamy grains; rice salads.

Cultivation: Pavese, lower Vercellese and Lomellina.

Arborio

This variety takes its name from the small town in the Vercellese region where it originated in 1946 as a derivation of the Vialone. Of all Italian rice, its grain is the largest and a certain skill is required to cook it homogeneously both inside and on the surface for a creamy risotto. It is perhaps the best-known and most widespread variety used for risottos.

▪ Features

Appearance: superfine rice, very fat grain (3-4 mm thick) with a length that can exceed 7 mm; rounded shape, with flat sides and very pronounced *tooth*.

Colour: whitish due to the presence of the large central pearl that almost occupies the whole grain. Absence of stripes.

Cooking: cooks in 13 minutes, with abundant release of starch and good absorption of aromas and flavours; granular to the tongue. Cooking point passes rapidly.

Taste: Starchy, low al dente consistency.

Use: creamy traditional mountain risottos; also good for soups and timbales.

Cultivation: Pavese, Ferrarese and Polesine.

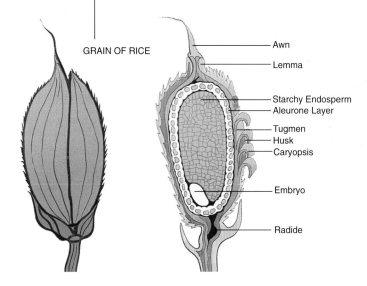

GRAIN OF RICE

- Awn
- Lemma
- Starchy Endosperm
- Aleurone Layer
- Tugmen
- Husk
- Caryopsis
- Embryo
- Radide

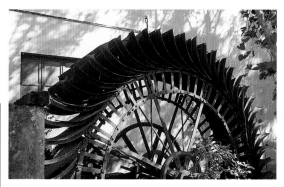

Baldo

This variety is becoming increasingly more popular due to its adaptability. It has replaced the Razza 77 and is grown on 10,000 hectares. According to two references, Baldo, together with many other varieties, are derived from the Lady Wright, a crossbreed with the original line of the national rice.

■ Features

Appearance: superfine rice, with fat grain up to 7 mm long; elongated, with flat regular sides, not very pronounced *tooth*.

Colour: cerulean and crystalline, with no pearl nor stripes.

Cooking: approx. cooking time 13 minutes, with low starch release, ample absorption of aromas and tastes; smooth to the tongue.

Taste: full and deliciously starchy.

Use: for creamy, oily risottos, mountain recipes with meat and/or cheese. Also for soups and oil cakes with vegetables.

Cultivation: Vercellese, Novarese and Lomellina.

Vialone enano

This rice is considered the origin of all prestigious rice varieties and, what is more, of the risotto. It was born in 1937 from the cross between Vialone and Nano (dwarf) and, unlike Carnaroli, Arborio and Baldo (all superfine), it belongs to the semifine category. It is the most versatile of the top-quality varieties and very popular among the most demanding gourmets.

■ Features

Appearance: semifine rice, with a medium thick, rounded and semi elongated grain; pronounced *tooth*, squashed head and rounded section.

Colour: white, with no stripes and a fairly big central pearl.

Cooking: cooking time 13 minutes, with abundant starch release, maximum absorption of aromas and flavours; creamy to the tongue. Maintains cooking

43

point.

Taste: the grains have a full and deliciously herbal taste and aroma. Medium *al dente* consistency.

Use: for risottos based on chicory, asparagus, pumpkin, snails and game.

Cultivation: Verona plain: (Bovolone, Buttapetra, Casaleone, Cerea, Concamarise, Erbé, Gazzo Veronese, Isola della Scala, Isola Rizza, Mozzecane, Nogara, Nogaole Rocca, Oppeano, Palù, Povegliano Veronese, Ronco all'Adige, Roverchiara, Salizzole, Sanguineto, San Pietro di Morubio, Sorgà, Trevenzueolo, Vigasio and Zevio).

Left: Old man drying rice, pencil, chalk and paint on laid paper, by Vincent Van Gogh, 1881.

Sant'Andrea

Another young, rising rice. Until recently was commercialised as Rizzotto. Rich in starch, often used for creamy rice dishes. Grains smaller than the Carnaroli, Arborio and Baldo varieties.

▪ Features

Appearance: fine rice, with medium length grain (6.6 mm), oval shape, blunt section and hardy perceptible *tooth.*

Colour: cerulean white with small central pearl. Small stripes.

Cooking: cooking time 15 minutes, with optimum yield; increases its volume about 5 times. Good absorption of aromas and tastes, smooth to the tongue. Medium *al dente* consistency; maintains cooking point..

Taste: starchy, slightly herbal, with firm, non elastic but granulous grain.

Use: all kinds of soups. Also good for thick only slightly creamy risottos.

Cultivation: mainly in the Baraggia region, and also in the north of the Vercelli plain.

Risotto:

from the pot to the plate

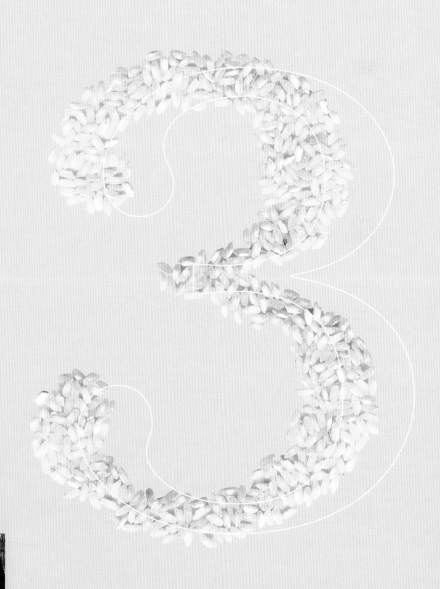

The abc of risotto

It is not known exactly when rice first appeared in Italy, but what is clear is that here - unlike eastern countries, where it was used simply as garnish and steam-cooked - rice has become an essential part of Italian cuisine in an endless variety of creative combinations. Risotto is of course historically associated with the Padana belt (Lombardy, Piemonte and Veneto), but it is gaining increasing popularity in the rest of the Italy in a wide range of recipes. What exactly is risotto? The Palazzi-Folena dictionary of the Italian language defines it as "a rice-based dish cooked with a little stock or juices, after having been lightly fried in butter with onion and aromatic herbs". The description is fairly clear and correct, but incomplete.

What rice should be used? And what about the stock? Is it added all at once or gradually? And the frying? Can one use olive oil or shallots? These doubts are reasonable, because under the general term "risotto" come dishes prepared in different ways, with very varied ingredients according to a wide range of traditions. Auguste Escoffier, considered the greatest chef of all times, defines the "risotto all'italiana" as a buttery soft and creamy risotto with separate grains obtained by adding butter or grated Parmesan at the end of the cooking and by stirring and blending the whole with a wooden spoon.

Some risottos, risotto *alla milanese* for example, are served "all'onda", that is, slightly liquid, with the grains separated from each other but united in a creamy whole. These risottos are traditional in Lombardy and Piemonte.

Many risottos recipes add vegetables, meat or fish, but not always at the beginning of the cooking. These ingredients can be cooked apart in another pan, and then added to the risotto halfway through or at the end of the cooking process.

What is needed
Frying pan or saucepan, wooden spoon, ladle for the stock.

The ingredients
Rice, butter, pure olive oil, onion, grated Parmesan (Parmigiano Reggiano).

Stages of risotto
1. Lightly fry ingredients
2. "Toast" the rice
3. Reduce the wine (optional)
4. Add the stock
5. Stir and blend
6. Cook
7. Add butter and/or Parmesan
8. All'onda

The pan
The pan must be wide-based. To prepare a risotto for four, use a pan with a 25 cm-diameter base and sides 10 cm high. The pan should be made of a good heat-conducting metal, such as tinned copper, aluminium (fairly thick) or steel.

The rice

The best varieties for risottos are Carnaroli, Roma, Baldo and Arborio in the superfine category and Vialone nano and Rosa Marchetti among the semifine varieties.

Onion

There are endless varieties of onions, which we will briefly classify as white, yellow, red and mild. Red onions have perhaps a more forceful taste and are not recommended when the recipe includes delicate ingredients, in which case mild onions are more appropriate. Shallots, with a delicate taste halfway between onion and garlic, also offer optimum results. And note that onions must be finely chopped and not "macerated" to the point of a liquid mass, impossible to fry.

Light fry (soffritto)

Some dishes require butter, others olive oil, and yet others both ingredients. It all depends, of course, on the recipe.

The amount of fat must not be overdone, otherwise the onion overfries. Sauté over moderate heat.

Put the butter or oil in the pan and add the chopped onion. If using butter, it is advisable to put the pan with the butter on the burner and the minute it has melted, add the onion. But if you use oil, add the onion when the oil is cold. In both cases, sauté the onion to a light golden colour. Now is the time to add the rice, an all-important moment insofar as flavour is concerned. It is essential not to roast it otherwise the risotto will have a roasted taste.

For some rice dishes, for example in fish-based recipes, a clove of garlic can be added and then later taken out so that its dominating note does not mask other flavours.

"Toasting" the rice

Toast the rice on a moderate fire. If the heat is too high, the rice will burn. This operation allows the rice to lose moisture, to absorb the condiments, to retain its perfume and to "reinforce" it (with this technique the grains remain whole and do not break during cooking).

Add the rice to the sautéed ingredients in the pan, over a moderate heat, and fry for a minute, stirring gently with a wooden spoon to allow each grain of rice to heat. In recipes which include other sautéed ingredients as well as onion, the frying stage can be prolonged to two or three minutes.

The wine

At this point many recipes add half a glass of wine. The effect is impressive: everything starts crackling and a deliciously perfumed steam comes from the wine, the rice and the ingredients in the pan. The wine evaporates; this is called *sfumare*, literally, "consume in smoke" meaning that the wine evaporates while depositing its flavours in the pan.

The stock

While preparing the risotto, the stock must be simmering on another burner (after bringing it to the boil, turn the heat down and maintain at constant temperature). The surface of the stock must be quietly simmering.

When the wine has evaporated, take a standard wooden ladle, fill it with hot stock and pour this over the rice. Stir with a wooden spoon to avoid the rice sticking to the bottom of the pan. One ladleful should be enough to cover the rice. If not, add half a ladle more. Note that the rice must not "float" but be covered by a couple of centimetres of stock. The visual effect is that the upper part of what we have been cooking bubbles gently. Keep the heat moderate.

Continue the cooking, and when most of the stock has been absorbed by the rice, add another ladleful. Continue in this way until the cooking is completed; a risotto needs to absorb a ladleful of stock at a time.

Stirring

Some say that a risotto should be stirred continuously, but this can ruin the dish and, in fact, is not necessary.

If the heat is kept moderate and a ladleful of stock is added before the previous one has been completely absorbed, the rice does not stick to the bottom of the pan. As a general rule, stir the rice gently each time you add the stock.

Al dente cooking

How long should the risotto cook? Two factors must be taken into account. The first is the type of rice. Carnaroli requires a little more time, Vialone nano, less. As an average, a risotto is cooked between 15 and 18 minutes. The second factor, *al dente*, means that the rice must have a firm centre to the bite. Just how firm depends on personal preferences. For the Piemontese, for example, this means really hard - to the point when at times the rice appears to be raw. Here is a tip on the subject: 14 minutes after adding the first ladleful of stock, taste it. If you find it still too firm let it cook another minute and check again. Still hard? Cook for a minute more. When you think the rice is almost ready and just needs half a minute more, add the final ingredients.

What should the risotto look like at this point? The rice should not be swimming in stock, but should still be moist.

Salting
When checking the rice taste it for salt at the same time. Add a little if necessary, but remember that if in the recipe Parmesano Reggiano is added during the final stage (*mantecatura*) the risotto will end up with a stronger taste.

Adding butter and/or Parmesan
Mantecare means mixing several ingredients together to give them a soft, creamy consistency. In the case of rice, these ingredients are grated Parmesano Reggiano and butter.

Proceed as follows: remove the pan from the heat, add the butter (in small pieces distributed over the whole surface of the risotto) then sprinkle with grated Parmesan. Mix gently but firmly with a wooden spoon.

One to two minutes are required for a good *mantecatura*, during which everything should amalgamate to produce the best risotto.

The grains should be united but distinguishable one from the other, firm to the bite and forming a smooth creamy whole.

"All'onda" risotto
This is the way Milanese risotto (among others) is served.

After adding the butter and grated Parmesan, the "all'onda" risotto is still quite liquid, with the grains loose but blended in a cream. The "onda" implies moving the pan back and forth to make a wave (onda) in the rice. This requires a little practice, but is not difficult. One can also add single cream to obtain the right creaminess (add two tablespoonfuls of cream during the *mantecatura*, but in this case reduce the amount of butter).

A tip from the chef

Many recipe books advise letting the risotto rest for a couple of minutes before serving. But the danger in this is the rice becoming a "porridge" or losing its *wave*. The best technique is to take the rice off the heat when it is *al dente* and moist (but not liquid). Let it rest for two minutes and only then add the final ingredients. In actual fact, the rice is not resting during these two minutes but absorbing the flavours even more.

The recipes

Unless otherwise stated, the recipes are for four people.

Cooking times for risottos are not specified for the reasons mentioned under the heading "*Al dente* cooking".

In general, risottos cook in 15-18 minutes from the moment of adding in the first ladleful of stock.

The stock should always be added boiling.

Salt: always check the rice for salt at the end of the cooking, and if required, add a little. We do not remind you to do this in every recipe and take it as understood.

The spoon used to mix the rice must always be made of wood.

Risottos are cooked with the pan uncovered, unless otherwise specified.

Serving the rice sprinkled with Parmesano Reggiano or another ingredient means that the risotto is put on the plates (if possible, heated) with the ingredient sprinkled on top.

The Stock

If a good glass of wine cheers the spirit and revitalizes the body, the same can be said of a good bowl of stock. But to prepare a "good broth" is an art ... an art that is fading.

Home-made stock is out of fashion, probably because it requires time; few people these days have three hours to spare for cooking and increasingly use glutamate-based cubes, whereby both our cuisine and our palates lose the nuances of "a good broth", overridden by the unmistakably uniform taste of glutamate.

But the effort is really worth it. Actually, stock can be left to make itself, there in the kitchen, in the evening, while you get on with something else. Just check it from time to time to skim it and there you are.

Stock is a very important ingredient of a good risotto: it gives it taste and flavours, and helps the rice to become a risotto by uniting the grains. And perhaps the secret of risotto lies precisely in the stock, and to a surprising degree.

Every cook has of course his or her secret recipe. Just by varying the meat cuts, the amount of a certain spice, by adding rosemary or not and the stock changes in substance and the risotto its nuances. Indeed, a whole thesis could be written on stock, but we will just offer the basic recipes, inviting you to modify them according to your fantasy.

The first Italian risottos were cooked with just hot water. In 1891, Pellegrino Artusi, in *Scienza in cucina e l'arte di mangiar bene* ("The science of cooking and the art of eating well") mentions hot water to prepare risotto with mushrooms or with peas. Only in the recipe for risotto *alla milanese* is meat stock mentioned.

Since then cooking has evolved and enriched, and risotto is definitively related to stock, now one of its essential ingredients.

The stock can be made with meat, chicken or vegetable, but court-bouillon and fish stock are also used. We explain how to prepare these broths and offer a few prescriptive rules.

Meat Stock

Place all the ingredient in the pot and cover with cold water. To calculate the amount of water, the general rule is to cover the meat and add approximately 7 to 10 cm (four fingers) more. However, the recipes indicate the quantity of water needed.

Bring to the boil on medium heat.

When the water boils, reduce heat to minimum: the stock should boil gently, with the surface of the water just simmering.

During cooking, remove the scum with a skimmer but it is not necessary to stir the stock. Add a little salt when cooking is completed: the meat and vegetables provide sufficient taste and flavours.

Cooking time: three hours. If time is not available you may use a pressure cooker (although genuine stock lovers may be horrified), which is certainly preferable to using meat cubes for your risotto stock.

Depending on the pieces and cuts of meat used, the meat stock will turn out more or less fat. Before using it for the risotto, the stock should be de-fatted. The simplest way is to refrigerate the stock for a couple of hours. The layer of solid fat that appears on the surface can then be easily removed with a kitchen slice.

If you follow the recipes below you will obtain much more stock than necessary to prepare a risotto for four people. This is intentional, because a greater quantity of water will allow you to use more pieces of different meat; in addition, the quantity of stock necessary to cook the risotto varies according to the type of rice used (some require longer cooking and, therefore, more stock) and also according to the intensity of the heat (if very high, more liquid is consumed). Another important aspect is the altitude; this may seem strange, but at over 1000 metres above sea level cooking rules change and, in the specific case of risotto, a greater quantity of stock will be needed. Finally, cooks always make slightly more stock than is needed, because "a good stock" always comes in use. It keeps in the refrigerator for a few days or can be frozen.

Ingredients for 3 litres of meat stock

- 1 kg mixed veal: neck, back, breast tip, ribs, lean pieces of choice
- 1 ox bone
- 1 marrow bone about 5 cm long
- 1 large onion
- 1 unpeeled garlic clove
- 2 celery stalks with leaves, cut in half
- 2 medium carrots, cut in half
- 1 potato (optional, makes the stock cloudy)
- 1 ripe tomato
- 3 juniper berries (optional)
- 2 cloves (optional)
- 5 grains of black pepper
- salt

Rinse the meat under the cold water tap and place it, together with the bones, in a 7-litre capacity pan. Stick the cloves, the juniper and the pepper in the onion and add to the meat with the rest of the vegetables.

Cover with 4.5 l cold water. Bring to the boil on moderate heat then reduce the heat to minimum and leave to cook for 3 hours. While the stock is boiling, skim the scum off the surface. When cooking is completed, taste and add salt if necessary.

Sieve and put aside the meat (which can be used in another recipe, e.g. Meatballs).

Refrigerate the stock for about 2 hours, then remove the solid fat formed on the surface with a skimmer or wooden spoon.

Chicken stock

"Old hen, good stock" say our grandmas. And it is true. But if you can get a good chicken, then fine, although a stock made with hen has a more delicate taste.

Ingredients for 3 litre hen or chicken stock.

- 1 hen (2 kg maximum), cleaned and ready to cook.
- 2 celery stalks with leaves.
- 2 medium carrots
- 1 onion
- salt

Put the hen whole in a large pan, add the celery, the carrots cut in halves and the onion.

Cover with 4 l of cold water. Bring to the boil on moderate heat. Reduce heat and cook for 3 hours. The surface of the water should simmer gently.

When cooking is completed, taste and add salt if

necessary.

Sieve and put the meat aside.

Refrigerate for a couple of hours and remove the solidified fat from the surface.

Vegetable stock

This stock has a delicate flavour and is easy to prepare. In addition, with a little practice, you can vary the ingredients according to personal preferences; for example, increasing the amount of carrots will produce a sweeter stock, while adding fennel root leaves will give it a particular flavour. If, on the other hand you wish to surprise your guests with a pink risotto, add five red cabbage leaves to the stock. The liquid will turn red (but the stock will not taste of cabbage) and the risotto will come out pink.

Ingredients for approx. 1.5 litres vegetable stock

- 2 spoonfuls extra virgin olive oil
- 1 onion
- 1 leek
- 1 carrot
- 1 celery stalk with its leaves
- 1 potato
- 1 courgette
- 1 tomato
- half a chilli (or a third)
- 1 bay leaf
- 1 clove
- salt

Wash and peel the vegetables and cut them into four pieces. Place the chilli and the wet vegetables in a large pan with the olive oil. Brown for 5 minutes on low heat with the lid on, stirring occasionally.
Add 2 litres of hot water, the bay leaf and clove, salt and cook on low heat for an hour.
Sieve the stock and remove the vegetables.

Court-bouillon

This stock is used in fish-based recipes. It includes the use of *bouquet garni*, made up of parsley (twenty small sprigs with their leaves), thyme (2 small fresh sprigs), one bay leaf and half a celery stalk, all tied in a bunch.

Ingredients for 2 litres of court-bouillon

- 400 g finely chopped onion
- 600 g carrot cut in thin slices
- 2 *bouquets garni*
- 2 coffee spoonfuls coarse sea salt
- 2 coffee spoonfuls white pepper grains

Place all the ingredients in the pan and cover with 2 l of cold water.

Bring to the boil on moderate heat. Cook for five minutes. The vegetables will be *al dente*. Sieve through a fine sieve before using.

Fish stock

To prepare a fish stock, different types of fishbones can be used (the fillets will of course be used in another recipe), but sole and turbot are popular choices. For *bouquet garni*, see recipe court-bouillon.

Ingredients for 2 litres of fish stock

- 1 kg. fishbones
- 60 g butter
- 2 *bouquets garnis*
- 100 g finely chopped onion
- 20 small parsley sprigs
- 1 sliced celery stalk
- salt

Clean and thoroughly wash the fish and place it in the pan. Add 2 l of cold water and bring to the boil on moderate heat.

Remove the scum with a skimmer. When the water boils add the vegetables and the bouquets garnis. Cook on moderate heat for half an hour.

Before using, strain through a fine sieve.

Parmesan Risotto

*t*his dish is not traditional of Parma, so it would be more correct to call it "risotto al parmigiano", because its name and its flavour come specifically from the cheese Parmigiano Reggiano. It is the most classical of all risottos. Once you have learned how to make this one, all other risottos will be "at your spoon's tip". So much so that in many recipe books it is called "Risotto all' italiana" and consists basically in lightly frying onions and browning the rice which is then cooked to absorb the stock.

Ingredients

- 350 g Arborio or Carnaroli rice
- 100 g butter
- half finely chopped onion
- 1,5 litres hot meat stock
- 50 g grated Parmigiano Reggiano

- Lightly fry the chopped onion till golden in half of the butter and, before it gets any browner, add the rice.
- Sauté the rice for a minute while stirring and then add a ladleful of boiling stock. When the stock is absorbed, add another ladleful and stir. Gradually add the stock as it is absorbed until the rice is cooked.
- When it is cooked, take it off the heat, stir in the remaining butter and parmesan.
- The risotto can be served with a sprinkling of parmesan.

Parmesan

Parmigiano Reggiano is produced in the provinces of Modena, Reggio Emilia, Parma, Bologna and Mantua using the milk from two different milkings. The afternoon milk is left to rest over night. The next morning, after removing surface fat, the recently milked whole milk is added to it. The subsequent caseification processes include the addition of lactic ferments, coagulation, cooking of the paste and brine salting of the cheeses. The last stage of this long process is the lengthy maturation lasting at least twelve months (sometimes even longer). The end product is much more than a "semifat cowmilk cheese of cooked paste, slow maturing, cylindrical and slightly convex ": it is the Parmigiano Reggiano, an essential cheese.

Recommended wine

Torgiano bianco

Grapes *trebbiano 50-70%, grechetto 15-35%, others 15%*

Region *Umbria*

Milanese Risotto

A t the beginning of the nineteenth century, the basic ingredients of this Milanese dish were rice, saffron, *cervellata* and Lodigiano cheese. *Cervellata* was a sausage made with pancetta fat, marrow, Parmesan, cinnamon, clove and nutmeg stuffed in saffron-dyed pig gut. *Cervellatas* are not made any more and Lodigiano, the seeding cheese of Lodi, is currently a rare treat, with only one producer left. Without its original ingredients, all that remains of the old *risotto alla milanese* is its yellow colour. There are many recipes, with small variations. We propose our own which, in respect for tradition, does not include wine.

Saffron

Saffron (Crocus sativus) is a very rare and expensive spice, at times reaching the exorbitant price of aprox. two thousand five hundred pounds sterling per kilo. To obtain one kilo of saffron two hundred thousand flowers are necessary, the equivalent to four hundred working hours. Production begins in August, when the bulbs are transplanted. The flowers are picked in October, at dawn, before the sun has had time to open them. The flowers are then opened (defloration), the petals, stamens and anthers discarded and the stigmas (three per flower) are kept and dried at the heat of live coals of an open fire. Finally, the saffron is crushed or preserved in threads. The most appreciated variety comes from the plateau of Navelli (Abruzzo) and from Turri, province of Cagliari (Sardinia).

Ingredients

- 350 g Carnaroli or Arborio rice
- 30 g butter
- 50 g chopped beef marrow
- 1 small chopped onion
- 1,5 litres hot meat stock
- 3 pinches saffron threads
- 1 dl. single cream (or fresh milk)
- 50 g grated parmesan

- Melt the butter with the marrow in a pan; add the chopped onion, brown lightly then add the rice and sauté it for a minute, stirring gently.
- Add the stock one ladle at a time, allowing it to be absorbed by the rice before adding the next ladleful.
- Dissolve the saffron in 1 dl of lukewarm stock and add to the rice 5 minutes before cooking is completed.
- When the rice is almost cooked, add the cream and the Parmesan and stir.
- This typical Milanese risotto must be served "all'onda ", that is, liquid but creamy, with loose firm grains.

Recommended wine

Barbera d'Asti

Grapes *barbera*
Region *Piedmont*

Asparagus Risotto

Risotto *de sparasi* is a traditional Venetian dish but other asparagus-growing regions of Italy - which produces white, green and violet varieties, all good for cooking with rice - have their own asparagus recipes. For the best results, the asparagus should be extremely fresh; to make sure, when broken they must make a dry, "crispy" sound.

Ingredients

- 300 g semifine rice
- 1 tender onion
- 60 g butter
- 3 tablespoons extra virgin olive oil
- 1 kg. fresh asparagus
- 1 litre hot chicken stock
- 3 tablespoons grated Parmesan

Asparagus

There are several different varieties of asparagus which we will briefly classify according to their colour. White asparagus owe their pallor to having been picked before they break the surface of the soil. The best-quality Italian varieties are produced in Bassano del Grappa, Rivoli Veronese, Cologna Veneta, Cimadolmo, Morgano, Badoere and Tavagnacco. The leading foreign white varieties are Ulma (or German White), Erfurt White, the 2001, Arak and the Dutch white.

In addition to the Italian white asparagus, almost all produced in the Veneto region, the best green variety is Altero, grown in the Bassa Ferrarese. The violet variety grows in Albenga (also known as "pink"), Milan (or Alemagna), Arcole in the Veronese, and around Naples.

- Clean and wash the asparagus and cut the tips, that is, keeping the most tender, non-fibrous upper part of the stem.
- Put the oil, half the butter and the onion in a pot and leave to brown slightly.
- Add the asparagus tips and leave to absorb flavour for 4 minutes, stirring occasionally.
- Add the rice, stir and leave to sauté for 2 minutes.
- Add a ladle of hot stock and stir; when the stock is absorbed, add another ladleful; continue in this way till the end of cooking.
- When the risotto is almost ready, remove from the heat, add remaining butter and Parmesan: stir and serve *all'onda*.

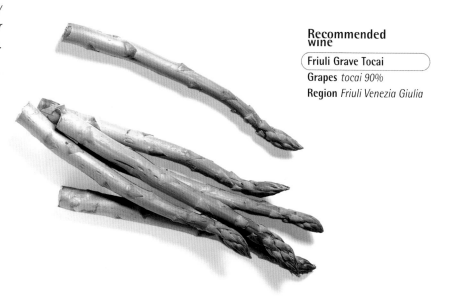

Recommended wine

(Friuli Grave Tocai)

Grapes *tocai 90%*
Region *Friuli Venezia Giulia*

Mushroom Risotto

Mushrooms are not the jewels in top chefs spectacular recipes like truffles are, but their unmistakable flavour still plays a major role in cooking, in particular when combined with rice, where each grain takes on their characteristic flavour. The best mushrooms for risottos are porcini mushrooms or cepes (*boletus edulis*), but extraordinary results are also obtained with *chiodini* and *galletti*. In this recipe, porcino mushrooms are used together with *Amanita caesarea*, which are often served raw.

Ingredients

- 300 g superfine rice
- 3 tablespoons of extra virgin olive oil
- 60 g butter
- 2 garlic cloves
- 100 g porcini mushrooms
- 100 g amanita caesarea
- 1,5 litres hot meat stock
- 1 tablespoon finely chopped parsley
- freshly ground white pepper

Alternative with dried mushrooms

- 350 g superfine rice
- 3 tablespoons of extra virgin olive oil
- 60 g butter
- 2 garlic cloves
- 40 g dried porcini mushrooms
- 1,5 litres hot meat stock
- 1 tablespoon finely chopped parsley
- freshly ground white pepper

- Leave the mushrooms to soak in hot water for half an hour. Strain them, put the water aside and roughly prick the mushrooms. Sieve the water to eliminate soil and other impurities.
- Put the olive oil, half the butter and the garlic in a pot and lightly fry on moderate heat.
- When the garlic starts browning, add the mushrooms and leave them to absorb flavour for 2 minutes, stirring occasionally. Add the rice and toast it for 2 minutes.
- Add the water used for soaking the mushrooms and cook for 2 minutes, stirring from time to time. Add a ladleful of hot stock and stir; remove the garlic.
- When the stock is almost all absorbed, add another ladleful, and continue in this way until cooking is completed. At this point, add the remaining parsley and butter and stir.
- Sprinkle ground white pepper over the risotto before serving (optional).

- Scrape the earth off the mushrooms, wash them under the tap and cut them in fine slices.
- Put the oil, half the butter and the garlic in the pot and lightly fry over moderate heat. When the garlic starts browning, add the rice and sauté it for a minute.
- Add a ladleful of hot stock and stir. Remove the garlic.
- When all the stock is almost absorbed, add another ladleful; continue gradually, a ladleful at a time, until cooking is completed.
- 7 minutes after adding the first ladleful of stock, add the mushrooms.
- At the end of cooking, add the remaining parsley and butter and stir.
- Serve the risotto sprinkled with freshly ground white pepper (optional).

Recommended wine

Pinot grigio

Grapes *pinot grigio 90%*
Region *Friuli Venezia Giulia*

Pumpkin Risotto

Pumpkins - a produce to be found in the vegetable gardens of rich and poor alike - have been used in cooking for centuries. The pumpkin is a simple food, but its simplicity and delicate sweetish flavour enhance any dish that includes it, such as fritters, gnocchi and, of course, risotto. To taste is to believe.

Ingredients

- 300 g Arborio rice
- 50 g butter
- 3 tablespoons of extra virgin olive oil
- 1 small chopped onion
- 500 g yellow pumpkin
- 1,5 litres hot vegetal stock
- 40 g grated Parmesan
- freshly ground black pepper

Pumpkins

What type of pumpkin does one use for risotto? There are indeed an extremely wide variety of pumpkins (ninety categories and nine hundred species) and not all are appropriate for cooking. The best Italian varieties are Marina di Chioggia, Piacentina and Mantovana. When buying a pumpkin, make sure it is whole, without soft or rotten areas. The pulp must be firm and floury, bright yellow or orange, without greenish nuances.

- Clean the pumpkin by removing all its inner fibres and skin; cut the pulp in small dices.
- Sauté the onion in the oil and half the butter. When it starts browning, add the pumpkin dices; cook for 8 minutes on moderate heat and stir to allow the pumpkin to "dry out" and absorb flavour.
- Add the rice and sauté it for 2 minutes.
- Add a ladleful of stock and stir. When the stock is almost completely absorbed, add another ladleful. Continue like this, a ladleful at a time, until cooking is completed.
- When the rice is cooked, remove from the heat, add the remaining butter and the Parmigiano Reggiano and stir. The sweet flavour of the pumpkin can be reduced by sprinkling freshly ground black pepper over the risotto.

Recommended wine

> Rosso dell'Oltrepò pavese

Grapes *barbera 25-65%; croatina 25-65%; uva rara, ughetta and pinot negro alone or mixed, max. 45%*

Region *Lombardy*

Seafood Risotto

Mussels, clams, winkles, shellfish, lobsters... the oceans contain more than eighty thousand species of seafood. Italian waters are no exception, and each coast area has its own recipes, in particular in the north.

However, in traditional recipes a single type of seafood or crustacean is used. Veneto, a traditional rice-growing area, has its Risotto *con i peoci* (mussels) and Risotto *con i caperozzoli* (molluscs). Friuli Venezia Giula specializes in rice with lobsters. And there are endless variations of risottos with clams. If you start with our recipe, soon you will be able to create your own personal risotto with your favourite seafood.

Ingredients

- 300 g Roma rice
- 300 g clams
- 300 g mussels
- 200 g small lobsters
- 1 bay leaf
- 6 tablespoons extra virgin olive oil
- 1 garlic clove
- 1 shallot
- 1 dl white wine
- 1 litre hot fish stock
- 2 tablespoons chopped parsley
- freshly ground black pepper

Seafood

Seafood used in cooking can be divided into three groups: bivalve shells (mussels, clams), single shells (sea snails, murex) and those with no, or an internal, shell (octopus, cuttlefish). Like any produce of the sea, they must be fresh. Make sure the shells are shiny and, in the case of bivalves, well closed; open valves mean they are not fresh. Smell them, the scent must be light and pleasant; if it is intense it means the shells left the sea too long ago. Finally, remember to wash the shells thoroughly under running water before cooking them. When you buy crustaceans, check their colour (must be bright and shining) and eyes (turgid and prominent when fresh).

- Scrub the mussels and clams and wash them under the tap. Put the seafood in a wide-based pan and turn up the heat. Stir with a wooden spoon until all the shells are heated: in 2 to 3 minutes they will open or half-open, releasing their "water". Sieve the liquid and put it aside. Remove the valves from the seafood.

- Strain the liquid obtained from the seafood through a fine cloth to eliminate the sand.

- Dry the lobsters and cut them roughly.

- Prepare the risotto by finely chopping the shallot and garlic (if you do not like the taste of garlic, leave the clove whole and cut it after browning the rice). Put everything in a pan with the oil and lightly fry on moderate heat.

- When the garlic and shallot start browning, add the rice, the clams, the lobsters and the mussels, and sauté for 2 minutes.

- Add the wine. Let it evaporate and then add the sieved seafood water. When this is almost completely absorbed, add a ladleful of hot fish stock.

- As the liquid is absorbed, add another ladleful of fish stock, and continue thus, one ladle at a time, until the rice is cooked.

- Finally add the chopped parsley and, if you wish, the black pepper.

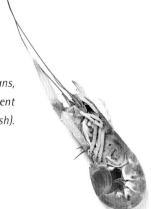

Recommended wine

(**Vermentino di Sardegna**)
Grapes *vermentino 85%*
Region *Sardinia*

Risotto with cuttlefish ink

Both the colour and the flavour of this dish will produce surprise and astonishment - two irresistible arrows shot straight to the heart of gourmets by a single archer: cuttlefish ink. This Florentine recipe originally appears in Pellegrino Artusi's *Scienza in cucina e l'arte di mangiare bene*. Artusi explains that cuttlefish are "called calamari in Florence perhaps (the beautiful Tuscan language often basing its words on similarities) because it houses a small sac (provided by nature as self-defence) containing a black liquid that can be used as ink".

Ingredients

- 300 g Vialone Nano rice
- 2 very fresh cuttlefish (approx. 700 g)
- 1 dl extra virgin olive oil
- half chopped onion
- 1 chopped garlic clove
- 1 dl white wine
- 1 tablespoon concentrated tomato sauce
- salt and freshly ground pepper

- Separate the head (the part with the tentacles) from the body of the cuttlefish by pulling hard. The viscera, that are joined to the head, will also come out, including two sacs, one a dark yellow colour and the other black, containing the ink. Handle this one gently and put it aside. Discard the rest of the viscera.

- Remove the eyes and the "mouth" (at the base of the tentacles) from the head. Open the body and extract the bone. Wash the cuttlefish well and cut the tentacles into small pieces and the body in 1 cm thick slices.

- Proceed to make the risotto. Put the olive oil, the garlic and the onion in a pot and fry lightly till golden.

- Add the cuttlefish and brown them for 5 minutes. Add the wine; when it has evaporated, add the concentrated tomato diluted in a ladle of hot water. Cover the pot and cook on low heat for half an hour, stirring occasionally.

- Add the rice, stir and let it absorb the juice of the cuttlefish. In the meantime, bring 1 l of water to the boil and salt it.

- When the rice is almost dry, add a ladle of boiling water and stir. When the rice has absorbed almost all the water, add another ladle and continue in this way until cooking is completed.

- When risotto is almost ready, add the ink of the cuttlefish and stir.

- Finally, check taste, add salt if necessary and a little freshly-ground white pepper if desired.

Recommended wine

Trebbiano d'Abruzzo

Grapes *trebbiano d'Abruzzo (bombino white) and/or trebbiano toscano, minimum 85%*

Region *Abruzzo*

Risotto with sausage and beans

The story goes that the Spanish explorers to the New World brought back some South American beans which they presented to their king, Carlos V. The king gave them to his noblemen, who in turn distributed them among their peers. Thus, from hand to hand, gift to gift, they found their way to Lamon, in the Veneto, where the farmers planted them and managed to produce two varieties: *lamon* and *borlotti*, from the dialect form *borlot*, meaning rounded. Country folk traditionally used borlotti beans in soups and also in rice dishes, such as Vercelli *panissa* or Novara *paniscia*. It is therefore not surprising to find them among the ingredients of a risotto.

Ingredients

- 300 g semifine or superfine rice
- 4 tablespoons extra virgin olive oil
- half chopped onion
- 2 bay leaves
- 100 g sausage, skinned and chopped
- 1 dl white wine
- 1,5 litres hot meat stock
- 200 g of soaked borlotti beans
- freshly ground white pepper

- Sauté the onion with the bay leaves in the oil. When the onion starts browning, add the sausage; stir for 5 minutes.
- Add the rice and sauté it for 1 minute, then add in the wine and leave it to evaporate.
- Add a ladleful of stock and stir; when the stock is almost completely absorbed, add another ladleful and wait till it is absorbed. Continue in this way until cooking is completed.
- Halfway through cooking, add the beans.
- When the rice is ready, sprinkle with white pepper and serve.

Beans and sausages

Beans have been cultivated for thousands of years all over the planet and there are more than a hundred and fifty different species. But bean dishes generally call for those from a specific region. In the Paniscia novarese, for example, Saluggia beans must be used. Lamon beans are among the most popular variety; they are similar to Borlotti, but smaller. Sausages are a widespread pork product where the meat and the fat are more or less finely minced and blended. Sausages vary from region to region depending on the different spices and other ingredients used in their making. In Mantova, for example, they contain salt, pepper, garlic and white wine; in Tuscany garlic and pepper predominate; in the Treviso area they smell of coriander and nutmeg; and Neapolitan sausages are extremely peppery.

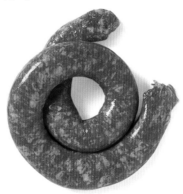

Recommended wine

Chianti classico DOCG

Grapes *sangiovese 75-100%; canaiolo 10%; trebbiano toscano and white malvasia, max. 10%*
Region *Tuscany*

Risotto with gorgonzola

*t*his is how it is said Gorgonzola cheese was born: one day, somebody unintentionally mixed the curd of the night milking with freshly milked curd in a wooden container. Needless to say, each curd had a different "personality" - different thickness and temperature. They tried to blend but found it impossible. Cracks formed and the serum, stagnating, became mouldy (in a process called *erborinatura*) - a green mould of unpleasant smell but delicious taste. Gorgonzola cheese had been born.

Ingredients

- 350 g Vialone Nano rice
- 40 g butter
- 1 small onion, chopped
- 1 dl white wine
- 1,5 litres boiling chicken stock
- 300 g sweet Gorgonzola
- 3 tablespoons of single cream

Gorgonzola

This cheese takes its name from the Lombardy town where it was born, Gorgonzola. It is a creamy cheese, of unmistakable aroma and flavour, with characteristic stripes produced by the formation of vegetable mould. The deeper, darker and more numerous are these stripes, the sharper the Gorgonzola.

- Melt the butter in a pot; add the onion and lightly fry it.
- When the onion starts going brown, add the rice and sauté it for a minute stirring gently.
- Add the wine and let it evaporate. Add a ladleful of stock and stir. When the rice has absorbed the stock, add another ladleful and stir. Continue adding the stock, a ladleful at a time, until the rice is cooked.
- Just before the end of cooking, add the Gorgonzola cut in small dices. Stir and blend gently.
- Remove the rice from the heat, add the cream and stir carefully.

Recommended wine

Cabernet franc

Grapes *cabernet 85%*
Region *Friuli Venezia Giulia*

Risotto with Barolo

J t is essential to have a good Barolo. Do not try this recipe with any other wine (unless it is a Brunello), because you risk preparing a risotto with a sour flavour that would not trigger in the palate the typical sensations of this Piedmont wine, very reliable where other wines could go "off". If we accepted "Old hen, good stock", then now we can say "Old Barolo, good rice". In other words, the recipe itself is simple: it is the Barolo that makes it special.

Ingredients

- 350 g superfine rice
- 80 g butter
- half chopped onion
- 1 bay leaf
- 4 dl Barolo wine
- 1 litre boiling meat stock
- 40 g grated Parmesan
- freshly ground white pepper

Barolo

Barolo is a town in the vineyard area surrounding Alba, and also the name of this ruby-red wine of intense, ample, rich aromas reminiscent of vanilla, chocolate, liquorice and spices. In ageing, this first-class Piedmont wine made with Nebbiolo grapes (from which Barbaresco and Gattinara are also obtained) acquires a garnet hue and almost always improves in both aroma and taste. Before going on the market, Barolo must age for three years and three months, two years at least of which are spent in oak and chestnut casks. Barolo Riserva, on the other hand, must age for five years and two months.

Is there a white wine comparable to Barolo that can be used in risottos? Yes, a sparkling Italian wine obtained according to traditional methods. If you make a risotto with sparkling wine, instead of a bay leaf add a little grated nutmeg.

- Lightly fry the chopped onion in half the butter with the bay leaf.
- When the onion begins to brown, add the rice, sauté it for a minute, add the wine at room temperature, reserving four tablespoons. Turn the heat up slightly to bring to the boil then turn it down.
- When the wine has evaporated, add the stock, a little at a time.
- At the end of the cooking, add the remaining butter and wine, the Parmesan and a little pepper.
- Serve the rice *all'onda*, sprinkling a little more Parmesan onto each dish.

Recommended wine

Nebbiolo d'Alba

Grapes *nebbiolo*
Region *Piedmont*

Vegetable Risotto

τhis dish should preserve all the fragrance of a vegetable garden in spring, so the risotto will be really exquisite if the vegetables are as fresh as possible. You can also have fun changing the ingredients for others of your choice depending on those available in each season. Or change the final touch by using, instead of fresh basil and parsley, other aromatic herbs such as mint, thyme, chives, chervil or wild fennel.

Broad Beans and Peas

Broad beans and peas have been enjoyed by gourmets from time immemorial. The Egyptians, the Greek and the Romans cultivated beans, and the first records on the use of green peas in the kitchen date back to 6000 BC, in Asia Minor. From the culinary point of view, peas have enjoyed wider popularity; ever since the sixteenth century when their delicate flavour won the favour of the élite and became a symbol of luxury and exquisiteness. The Sun King raved about them, in spite of complaints from his favourite, Madame de Maintenon. Apart from royal ravings, fresh peas cooked in water with small fresh onions (or ham or bacon), and raw broad beans with goats cheese (as in Tuscany) are exquisite dishes. But only when absolutely fresh are they at their best. So make sure their pods are firm before buying broad beans and peas.

Ingredients

- 300 g Roma rice
- 40 g streaky bacon
- 3 tablespoons extra virgin olive oil
- 2 shallots (or mild onions)
- 1 small carrot
- 1 celery stalk
- 400 g ripe tomatoes
- 1 small courgette
- 400 g fresh broad beans in their pods
- 300 g fresh green peas in their pods
- 1,5 litres boiling vegetable stock
- 3 tablespoons of grated Parmesan
- 5 basil leaves
- 1 tablespoon chopped parsley
- salt and freshly ground white pepper

- Chops the shallots, the carrot and the celery and place them in a frying pan with the oil and the bacon cut in small dices. Fry lightly on moderate heat stirring occasionally. In the meantime, pod the beans and peas.

- After 3 minutes, when the vegetables are well browned, add the tomatoes (without seeds), the marrow cut to small dice and the broad beans.

- Cook on a low heat for 20 minutes, stirring. If the vegetables dry too fast and stick to the bottom of the pan, add a tablespoon or two of stock.

- Add the peas and cook 10 minutes more. At this point all these ingredients should not be brothy; add the rice and sauté it for 1-2 minutes to give it time to absorb all the flavours.

- Add a ladleful of boiling stock and stir; continue cooking adding a ladle of stock whenever necessary.

- When the rice is cooked, remove from the heat, blend in the grated Parmigiano Reggiano and add the chopped parsley and basil (roughly torn into small pieces by hand).

- Sprinkle with freshly-ground white pepper and serve.

Recommended wine

Bianco di Custoza

Grapes *trebbiano toscano 20-45%; tocai friulano 5-30%, malvasia toscana, riesling italico, pinot bianco and chardonnay 20-30%, garganega 20-40%*

Region *Veneto*

Risotto with chicken livers _____

Since the mid-15th century Italian cuisine has included the use of chicken - and other birds'-livers both alone and with other giblets.

One of the most popular recipes with chicken livers is the *risotto alla sbirraglia*.

Ingredients

- 300 g Roma rice
- 30 g butter
- 1 small onion
- 1 small carrot
- half celery stalk
- 100 g chopped veal
- 150 g chopped chicken livers
- 400 g ripe tomato
- 1 dl white wine
- 1,5 litres boiling meat stock
- finely grated Parmesan

Chicken Livers

Make sure the chicken livers are very fresh. It is also very important to clean them well by carefully removing the bile sac, which tastes extremely bitter and would ruin the dish.

- Place the finely chopped onion, carrot and celery in a pot with the butter and sauté on moderate heat until the onion starts browning.
- Add the meat and the chicken livers and sauté for 2-3 minutes while stirring.
- Peel the tomatoes and cut them in small pieces removing the seeds; add them to the meat and cook on moderate heat for 10 minutes or until the tomato has absorbed all its liquid and is blended with the other ingredients.
- Add the rice and sauté it for 2 minutes while stirring; add the wine and give it time to evaporate, then add the first ladleful of hot stock.
- When the rice has absorbed almost all the stock, add another ladle and continue, a ladle at a time, until cooking is completed.
- Sprinkle grated Parmesan over the risotto and serve.

Recommended wine

Chianti DOCG

Grapes *sangiovese 75-100%, canaiolo negro 10%, trebbiano toscano and malvasia white max. 10%, others red max. 10%*

Region *Tuscany*

Seafood Risotto Viareggio Style

A s everybody knows, rice grows in water, and this is perhaps why it combines so well with fish and seafood. Jokes apart, its *sea rice* is truly a feather in the gastronomic hat of Viareggio, whose port hums early in the morning with the frenetic contracting between fishermen and restaurants or individuals. Indeed, the sea around Versilia is rich in unique squids, prawns, clams and tellins, which in the local tradition combine perfectly with both pasta and rice.

Ingredients

For the fish stock

- 500 g approx. of fish (venus shells, spider crabs, scorpionfish, red mullets, mackerel)
- 1 carrot
- 1 celery stalk with some leaves
- 1 garlic clove
- 1 bunch of basil
- half an onion
- 1 dl white Montecarlo wine
- 3 tablespoons extra virgin olive oil

For the risotto

- 200 g Carnaroli rice
- 200 g squids
- 200 g prawns
- 200 g red mullets
- 200 g sole
- 300 g cleaned clams
- 1,5 litres boiling fish stock
- 1 dl white Montecarlo wine
- 1 garlic clove
- half a chilli
- 1 tablespoon chopped parsley
- 3 tablespoons extra virgin olive oil
- salt and freshly ground black pepper

Recommended wine

(Montecarlo bianco)

Grapes *60-70% trebbiano toscano and/or semillon, pinot grigio*

Region *Tuscany*

- The fish stock: crush all the herbs and sauté in 3 tablespoons of olive oil in a large pot; add the wine and allow it to evaporate. Add the clean fish, washed and cut in pieces, and when they start coming apart, add sufficient water to cover them completely. Cook on a very low heat for about one hour and then strain and taste for salt.

- The risotto: wash and clean the squids and the clams, carefully fillet the red mullets and the soles, peel the prawns and remove their intestinal thread. Place the clams in a frying pan on strong heat to open them; remove them from the shells.

- Put 3 tablespoons of oil, the garlic and the chilli in a pot and heat. When the garlic starts browning, add the squid cut in small pieces, the prawns, red mullet, the sole and the clams. Add salt and pepper and brown; then add the white wine and allow it to evaporate.

- Add the rice, sauté for 1 minute and add a ladleful of hot stock. When the rice has absorbed almost all the stock, add another ladle; continue in this manner until the rice is cooked.

- Just before the end of cooking, add a little chopped parsley. .

Restaurant **Romano**
Via Mazzini, 120
Viareggio, Lucca

o *Massa*

Lucca

Viareggio

o *Pisa*

Risotto with frogs' legs

Jn several Italian regions frogs used to form the main dish of a meal. They were "hunted" near the irrigation canals and small lakes and cooked in different ways. It was inevitable that in a rice-growing area like Lomellina they ended up in a risotto. Frogs were, and still are, also used to make a good, tasty and very digestive stock, which was traditionally given to those suffering from respiratory problems.

Ingredients *For the frog stock*

- 500 g frogs' legs, cleaned
- 1 onion
- 2 carrots
- 2 celery stalks
- 1 handful of parsley
- 1 ripe tomato
- salt

For the risotto

- 300 g Carnaroli rice
- 150 g butter
- 1 small shallot, chopped
- 2 celery stalks, finely chopped
- 400 g frogs' legs, cleaned
- 3 dl white wine
- 1 ripe tomato
- 1 litre boiling frog stock
- 2 tablespoons grated cheese
- 1 branch parsley, finely chopped

Recommended wine

Oltrepò Pavese Pinot nero vinificato in bianco

Grapes *pinot nero 85%; others, max. 15%,*
Region *Lombardy*

- For the frog stock: place all the ingredients in 2 l of cold water in a large pot. Bring to the boil on moderate heat; when the water boils, reduce the heat to the minimum (the surface should barely simmer) and cook for 45 minutes.

- When the stock is ready, remove the vegetables and strain, crushing the frogs' legs.

- For the risotto, sauté the shallot and the celery in 70 g of butter and when they start browning, add the clean frogs and leave to brown for 5 minutes.

- Add the peeled and chopped tomato; add 2 dl of white wine, then put the lid on the pot and stew on a low heat for about 20 minutes.

- Cool and then patiently bone the frogs' legs. Discard the bones and reserve all the juice and the meat.

- In another pot, sauté the rice alone for a minute on a moderate heat.

- Add 1 dl of white wine and let it evaporate. Add the frogs' meat and juice and then the stock, a ladleful at a time, waiting for the previous one to be absorbed before adding the next one.

- At the end of the cooking, turn off the heat, add the remaining butter, the cheese and the parsley and blend.

Novara
Vercelli *Vigevano*
Ceretto
Lomellina *Mortara*
Pavia
Po

Rest. **Cascina Bovile**
Via Bovile, 2
Ceretto Lomellina, Pavia

Risotto with White Truffles _____

*J*magine the Piedmont, from Alba to Asti, wrapped in Autumn mists, close your eyes, breathe the damp air and remember the aroma of truffles. Then "see" a skilful hand cutting the fine white slices that are gently placed on the risotto. The intense and at the same time delicate perfume and flavour of white truffles are unmistakable; they enchant the palate. Indeed, it was possibly thanks to these qualities that the Romans considered truffles a product of the gods, with magical and aphrodisiac powers. On the latter, we reserve our opinion, but it certainly is magical.

Ingredients

- 300 g Carnaroli rice
- 50 g butter
- 1 small onion
- 6 rosemary leaves
- 1,5 litres boiling meat stock
- 60 g white Alba truffles
- 3 tablespoons grated Parmesan
- salt and black pepper

Recommended wine

(Dolcetto di Dogliani)

Grapes *dolcetto*

Region *Piedmont*

- Finely chop the onion; brown it in a pan in 30 g of butter and the rosemary.
- Add the rice and sauté it for 1 minute.
- Add a ladleful of boiling stock and stir. When the stock is almost completely absorbed, add another ladleful and wait till it is absorbed. Continue in this way until the end of cooking.
- When the rice is *al dente*, remove it from the heat and add 20 g of truffles cut in thin slices, the remaining butter and the grated Parmesan and blend.
- Taste for salt and pepper, spread the remaining truffle slices on each ration and serve.

Asti
Alessandria
S. Damiano
Nizza
Monferrato
Costigliole d'Asti
Alba

Restaurante **Da Guido**
Piazza Umberto I, 27
Costigliole d'Asti, Asti

Risotto with Peppers

traditional dish of the Upper Versa Valley in its country feastday version with veal or chicken fillets. Voghera peppers are square-shaped and light green and are cultivated in Lombardy between the towns of Voghera and Stradella. It is a local variety that only grows here and is not included in any official classification. It has a distinct taste, more savoury than the peppers grown in Asti (which are yellow or red), is of averaged thickness, very fleshy and medium size. It was used a lot in the past in oil or vinegar conserves, and also in dishes like this local Voghese risotto. Today this pepper has almost disappeared due to its poor resistance and a lack of interest in its cultivation.

Ingredients

- 350 g Carnaroli rice
- 3 peppers: one red Asti, one yellow Asti and one green Voghera
- 60 g butter in small pieces
- 3 shallots, finely chopped
- 2 garlic cloves
- 4 tablespoons of extra virgin olive oil
- 200 g veal or chicken fillets
- 100 g grated Parmesan
- 1,5 litres boiling meat stock
- salt and freshly ground black pepper

Recommended wine

(Oltrepò Pavese Bonarda)

Grapes *croatina 85-100%; other grapes, max. 15%*
Region *Lombardy*

- Blanch the peppers in boiling water for about two minutes; cool and skin them. Cut them in medium-sized pieces.

- Put 20 g of butter, the olive oil, the garlic, the chopped shallots, the paprika and meat cut in small pieces in a pan. Sauté on moderate heat for 8-10 minutes.

- Add the rice, sauté it for a couple of minutes and add a ladleful of stock; stir.

- When the stock is almost completely absorbed, add another ladleful, and continue, a ladleful at a time, until the end of cooking.

- When the rice is almost al dente, remove it from the heat, add the remaining butter, the grated cheese, pepper and blend well. Leave to rest for a minute before serving.

Pavia

Po

Stradella

Voghera

S.Maria d.Versa

Montecalvo Versiggia

Restaurant **Prato Gaio**
Via Versa, 16
Montecalvo Versiggia PV

Risotto with Gudgeons and Hops

Old Venetian recipe

two rather unusual ingredients go into this recipe. Gudgeons (*ghiozzo*) are small fish found in the Venetian lagoon, very appropriate for preparing fish stock. *Bruscandoli* are the budding hops that grow along the banks of streams. They are popularly known as wild asparagus and appear in March and April.

Ingredients *For the fish stock*

- 1 kg gudgeons
- 2 celery stalks
- 2 carrots
- 1 onion
- 1 ripe tomato
- salt

For the hops

- 1 kg budding hops
- 1 garlic clove
- half an onion, chopped
- 2 tablespoons of extra virgin olive oil

For the risotto

- 360 g Vialone Nano rice
- 30 g butter
- 3 tablespoons of extra virgin olive oil
- 1 dl white wine
- 1 tablespoon chopped parsley
- 2 tablespoons grated Parmesan
- 1,5 litres boiling gudgeon stock

- Pick out the four largest fish, cut off their heads and clean them. Cut into eight fillets; flour and fry. These will be used later to decorate the dish.

- Boil the rest of the fish, the celery, the carrot, the onion and the tomato for 20-30 minutes (like a normal meat stock) in 2-3 litres of salty water. Strain the stock while crushing the fish.

- Meanwhile, clean the hops keeping only the tender part (the tips and upper part of the stem); wash and cut them in small pieces.

- Lightly fry the onion and garlic clove; when they start browning, add the hops and sauté for 4-5 minutes (so they only half-cook).

- To prepare the rice: put a tablespoon of olive oil in a pan and heat gently. Add the rice and sauté it. Then cover with the wine and allow it to evaporate.

- Add a ladleful of hot gudgeon stock, stir and proceed by adding another ladleful from stock only when the previous one has been absorbed.

- 2 minutes before the end of cooking time, add the hops.

- When the rice is al dente, remove it from the heat, add the butter, Parmesan, parsley and, if you wish, two tablespoons of oil. Blend well.

This risotto must be served "*all'onda*", decorated with the fried gudgeon fillets.

Recommended wine

Lison Pramaggiore Tocai italico

Grapes *tocai italico, min. 90%; others, max. 10%*

Region *Veneto*

Treviso

● *Mestre*

Venezia

Trattoria **Dall'Amelia**
Via Miranese, 113
Mestre, Venecia

Risotto with Pork and Veal

*t*his risotto descends from the famous *risotto alla pilota*, which dates back to the sixteenth century when the first *pile* (equivalent to today's rice processing plants) were built in Veneto. The meal was prepared by the *piloti* or workers, with the lard given to them during the slaughtering season by the nobles who owned the *pile*.

Ingredients

- 400 g Vialone Nano rice
- 60 g butter
- 1 small sprig of rosemary
- boiling vegetable stock, double the amount of the rice
- 80 g pork chine
- 80 g lean veal
- 2 spoonfuls of brandy
- 60 g grated Parmesan
- cinnamon, in powder
- salt and freshly ground black pepper

Recommended wine

Valpolicella

Grapes *corvina veronese or corvina, 40 to 70%; rondinella, 20 to 40%; molinara, 5 to 25%; and/or rossignola, negrara trentina, barbera and sangiovese, max 15% others, max. 5%*

Region *Veneto*

- Melt the butter in a pan with the rosemary.
- When the butter is brown, take out the rosemary, add the meat cut in small dices and brown.
- Add the salt, pepper and brandy. Turn the heat down and cook the meat for 5 minutes.
- Place the rice in a pan and lightly fry on moderate heat for 1 and a half minutes.
- Add the boiling stock all at once, stirring gently. Cover and turn the heat down to minimum. Cook without stirring. (To calculate the amount of stock, measure the volume of the rice in a container such as a teacup: the amount of stock will be double this).
- Cook for 12 minutes then add the meat with the cooking juice and cover again without stirring.
- When the rice is cooked, turn the heat off, add the Parmesan and sprinkle with cinnamon. Blend gently and serve.

Verona

Adige

Isola della Scala

Mantova

Restaurant **Pila Vecia**
Via Saccovaner, 6
Passolongo di Isola della Scala, Verona

Yellow Risotto with Pig's Tail Stew

his is a traditional dish from the town of Crema in which the typical saffron-yellow Milanese risotto is combined with an unusual ingredient based on pork tail, symbol of this Padania region - although the saying "nothing of the pig is wasted" can be applied to all Italian cuisine from Trieste southwards. In this recipe, the tail, often accompanied by sauce, is particularly delicious - as well as digestive.

Ingredients *For the tail stock*

- 2 pig tails
- half an onion
- 1 celery stalk
- 1 carrot
- 1 bay leaf
- 15 g pork lard
- 2 shallots
- 1 garlic clove
- 1 dl dry white wine
- 200 g ripe tomato
- salt and black pepper

For the risotto

- 280 g Carnaroli rice
- 2 spoonfuls extra virgin olive oil
- 1 shallot
- 1 dl dry white wine
- 1,5 litres boiling meat stock
- 0,15 g saffron
- 3 spoonfuls grated Parmesan
- 15 g butter

- Cook the tails in salty boiling water for 50 minutes with the onion, half the celery stalk, half the carrot and the bay leaf.
- When the tails are cooked, separate the meat; cut the meat and the rind into dices.
- Finely chop the remaining onion, celery and carrot and brown in butter in an earthenware pan. Add the pieces of tail, cover with the wine and leave to evaporate. Add the peeled and chopped tomatoes. Cover with hot water and cook on moderate heat, stirring occasionally, for 30 minutes, checking salt and pepper.
- For the rice: lightly fry the chopped shallot in olive oil. When it starts to brown, add the rice and sauté all the ingredients for a minute. Add the white wine and let it evaporate.
- Add a ladleful of boiling stock and stir. When the stock is absorbed, add another ladleful; continue in this way until the rice is cooked.
- Halfway through the cooking, add the saffron dissolved in 1 dl of hot stock.
- At the end of cooking, remove from the heat, add the butter and the cheese and blend.
- Serve with the pork tail stew in the middle of the risotto.

Recommended wine

Dolcetto d'Ovada

Grapes *dolcetto*
Region *Piedmont*

Crema

Ripalta Cremasca

Lodi

Cremona

Codogno

Restaurant **Via Vai**
Via Libertà, 18
Località Bolzone
Ripalta Cremasca CR

Rice Bomb

The rice bomb is a dish for which the Parmese feel genuine passion. It is a rice timbale filled with young pigeon meat. Although the recipe is not originally from Parma, in this city it enjoys a solid and long-lasting reputation.

Ingredients *For the filling*

These amounts are for 6-8 people

- 4 spoonfuls extra virgin olive oil
- 4 young pigeons
- 3 garlic cloves
- 1 onion
- 1 celery stalk
- 2 bay leaves
- 2 dl white wine
- 1 spoonful of tomato sauce
- salt

For the risotto

- 600 g Vialone Nano rice
- 1 dl white wine
- 2 eggs
- 50 g grated Parmesan
- butter to grease the mould and decorate the timbale
- breadcrumbs to line the mould

- Clean and wash the pigeons thoroughly. Cut them in quarters.
- Put the olive oil, the garlic cloves, the onion, the roughly cut celery and the bay leaves in a pan and lightly fry for 3-4 minutes on moderate heat while stirring.
- When the ingredients start softening, add the pigeon quarters and brown for 2-3 minutes.
- Add the wine and let it evaporate. Add the tomato sauce and blend.
- Add 5 dl of hot water, salt and cook for 3/4 of an hour (same cooking technique as stewing).
- When the pigeons are cooked, cut them into small pieces without boning them.
- Remove the transparent oil released by the pigeon cooking juice and reserve for the risotto. Pass the rest of the juice through a potato masher, after removing the bay (and the garlic for those who find it indigestible).
- Now start preparing the rice: put the reserved oil in a pan, add the rice and sauté it for 2 minutes to give it time to absorb the flavours. Add the wine and let it evaporate.
- Slowly add the strained pigeon juice, adding more when the previous ladleful is almost completely absorbed. Cook in this way for 8 minutes, which is half the cooking time. Remove the smooth risotto from the heat, add the eggs and the Parmesan and blend. The result is a risotto *all'onda*.
- Grease a 25 cm diameter round mould with butter and sprinkle with breadcrumbs. Pour in a little more than half the rice making sure it adheres well to the bottom and sides of the mould. Place the pieces of pigeon in the centre forming a regular layer, cover with the rest of the rice and level the surface. Sprinkle breadcrumbs over the surface and spread small pieces of butter on top.
- Put the mould in the oven at 170° and cook for about 20 minutes, that is, until a golden crust forms on top.
- When the bomb is ready, leave for 5-10 minutes before de-moulding it.

Recommended wine

Friuli Collio Merlot

Grapes *merlot*
Region *Friuli Venezia Giulia*

Restaurant **Cocchi**
Via Gramsci, 16
Parma

Paniscia di Novara

O n important feastdays, especially in cold winters when Novara was wrapped in mist, there was always a *paniscia* on the country folks' table. This is of course a main dish, as it contains rice, pulses, vegetables and salami. The latter was, and still is, not just any salami but *salamin d'la doja*, a soft salami made with pork, spices, garlic and Barbera wine and preserved under a layer of lard dissolved in a terracotta barrel called *doja*.

Ingredients

For the vegetables

- 3 light-coloured onions, sliced
- 2 spoonfuls extra virgin olive oil
- 2 litres boiling vegetable stock
- 100 g tender Borlotti beans
- 100 g celery stalk
- 100 g carrot
- 100 g cabbage
- 100 g leek
- 100 g courgette
- 100 g fresh tomato pulp
- salt

For the paniscia

- 300 g Carnaroli rice
- 2 spoonfuls extra virgin olive oil
- 1 white onion, finely sliced
- 1 dl full-bodied red wine
- 120 g of salamin d'la doja
- 20 g pork rind, boiled and cut in thin slices
- 5 spoonfuls grated Parmesan
- black pepper, freshly ground

- Prepare the vegetables: put olive oil and the onion in a pan; when brown, add the vegetable stock.

- Add the vegetables "in progression", following the order in the list of ingredients, which takes into account cooking times of each. Start, therefore, with the beans, then cut the other vegetables in small dice and add them one by one to the pan. With this method the stewed vegetables preserve their colour and firmness. From the moment of adding the pulses, calculate 30 minutes cooking time. On completion, taste for salt.

- Then prepare the *paniscia*: put 2 spoonfuls of olive oil in the pan with the onion. When it starts browning add the salami (broken in small pieces by hand) and brown for 1 minute stirring all the time.

- Add the rice and sauté for 1 minute. Add the wine (the chef recommends Ghemme or Gattinara) and allow it to evaporate.

- Add the rinds, mix, and add 2 ladlefuls of the vegetable stew. Add another ladleful of stew as soon as the rice is almost dry.

- After about 15 minutes, remove from the heat, add the Parmesano Reggiano, one or two spoonfuls of olive oil, blend and serve the rice with a sprinkling of freshly-ground black pepper.

Recommended wine

(Gattinara)

Grapes *nebbiolo, vespolina, max. 4%; and/or bonarda di Gattinara, max. 10%*

Region *Piedmont*

°Arona

Borgomanero

°Busto Arsizio

°Novara

°Vercelli

Restaurant **Pinocchio**
Via Matteotti, 147
Borgomanero, Novara

Panissa di Vercelli

Once upon a time Nissa, the marquis of Vercelli's beloved wife, was unhappy because she was childless. One stormy day, a nobleman from the court took refuge in the humble house of a peasant family blessed with five lovely children. The mother, bending over a steaming pot, was expecting a sixth child. When questioned by the nobleman, the husband laughingly answered that all the credit should go to the only dish their poverty could afford, but one that was seasoned and prepared with sincere love. He then presented his guest with the steaming pot. The nobleman rushed out into the storm with his gift. When he got to the castle he managed to say the words "*Par la Nissa*, for Nissa" before falling exhausted onto the floor. The marquis and Nissa tasted that humble food and after nine months twins were born. The marquis went mad with joy, and the world came to know about *panissa*, a dish as simple as the people who cooked it and as generous as the land of its birthplace.

Ingredients

For the stock
- 70 g pork lard
- 1 onion
- 200 g dry Saluggini beans
- 3 or 4 bay leaves
- 1 pig's forefoot or prete (rolled rind)
- coarse salt

For the panissa
- 280 g Baldo rice
- 70 g pork lard
- 1 onion
- 1 dl red wine
- 100 g de salamin d'la doja (see pg. 98)
- extra virgin olive oil for dressing
- grated Parmesan
- black pepper, freshly grated

Recommended wine

Barbera d'Asti DOC

Grapes *barbera, min. 85%; freisa, grignolino, dolcetto, max. 15%*

Region *Piedmont*

Restaurant Da Balin
Frazione Castell'Apertole
Livorno Ferraris, Vercelli

- Soak the Saluggini beans (a Borlotto variety grown in Saluggia) for at least 4 hours.
- Mix the pork lard with the onion and lightly fry on moderate heat in a large pot. When the onion starts browning, add the beans and brown them for a minute, stirring.
- Add 4 l of cold water, 3 or 4 bay leaves, the pig's trotter, the *prete* and salt. When the water start boiling, turn the heat down to minimum and cook for an hour, making sure the stock simmers without boiling (in this way the beans stay firm).
- Then prepare the rice: fry the lard and chopped onion on medium heat. When the onion starts browning, add the rice and sauté for 1 minute.
- Add the wine (the chef recommends Barbera), let it evaporate and then add a ladleful of bean stock and stir. Break up the *salamin d'la doja* with your hands, and (optional) the *prete* cooked in the stock.
- When the rice is almost dry, add another ladleful of stock. Continue in this way, a ladleful at a time, until the end of the cooking. Note: not all the beans used in the stock are added to the *panissa*, in which rice is the predominating ingredient. The total amount of beans added should be equivalent to a ladleful.
- Cook until *al dente* and leave the *panissa* rather moist. Cover the rice and place the pot on a cold surface for 3-4 minutes. The rice will now be thicker (prod the *panissa* with a folk, it should remain upright).
- Serve with a little olive oil and a sprinkling of Parmesan and black pepper.

Risotto with Catfish and Chives

his traditional risotto includes catfish, which taste rather like carp or other freshwater fish, although tradition demands the specific use of catfish, enhanced by the spices and refreshed by the chives.

Ingredients

- 300 g Vialone Nano rice
- 2 catfish (total 400 g)
- 100 g white 00 flour
- 1 dl extra virgin olive oil
- 40 g butter
- half an onion
- a quarter salted anchovy
- nutmeg
- cinnamon, whole
- 3 dl boiling vegetal stock
- 4-5 threads chives
- salt and black pepper

Recommended wine

(Franciacorta bianco DOC)

Grapes *pinot bianco and/or chardonnay*

Region *Lombardy*

- Start by preparing the catfish: flour the fish and fry them in olive oil. Remove them and strain off the oil, peel them and remove head and backbone. Place the fish meat in a pan with half the butter and two or three onion slices. Flavour with a little grated nutmeg and a little cinnamon, salt and pepper.
- Add the anchovy (rinsed under running water to remove excess salt and broken in small pieces) and cook on moderate heat, stirring to blend all the ingredients, for 5 minutes.
- Now prepare the rice: lightly fry the finely chopped onion in the remaining butter. Add the rice and sauté it, stirring for a minute.
- Add a ladleful of boiling vegetable stock and stir; when the rice has absorbed almost all the stock, add another ladleful; continue in this way, a ladleful at a time, until the end of cooking.
- 3 minutes before the rice is cooked, add the fish dressing and, at the last moment, the chopped chives. Serve on well-heated plates.

Asola

Canneto s.Oglio

Oglio

Mantova

Cremona

Bozzolo

Sabbioneta

Restaurant **Dal Pescatore**
Località Runate
Canneto sull'Oglio MN

Cream Risotto with Veal Marrow

N ot everybody is familiar with marrow, perhaps because it is considered an inferior meat product. In Italy its name may vary according to the region. It is the spinal cord of beef, which in the Piemonte is used mainly for preparing *finanziera* (offal stew). Remove the outer skin and soak the pieces of marrow in cold water. Put them on the heat in cold water and take them out when the water starts to boil. They are now ready for a series of recipes.

Ingredients

- 300 g Carnaroli rice
- 3 spoonfuls extra virgin olive oil
- 1 chopped shallot
- 1,5 litres clear stock (i.e. prepared with lean veal)
- 150 g veal marrow
- 4 artichokes
- 1 spoonful chopped parsley
- 50 g butter
- 2 garlic cloves

Recommended wine

Bonarda Bric Millon

Grapes *bonarda 90%, barbera and dolcetto the remainig 10%*
Region *Piedmont*

- Put the oil in a pan and heat on moderate fire for a few seconds (before it fries or smokes). Add the rice, brown for 2 minutes; add the shallot and continue sauteing and stirring, until it is a light golden colour.
- Add a ladleful of boiling stock; stir. When the rice has absorbed almost all the stock, add another ladleful and continue in this way until end of cooking.
- Cook for 10 minutes. While the rice is cooking, clean the artichokes (only the hearts and the most tender central parts, are used) and place them in cold water with a few drops of lemon to prevent them from blackening. Cut the marrow (without its skin) into 3 cm-long pieces.
- After 10 minutes add the marrow to the rice and cook for 2 minutes.
- Add the finely sliced artichokes and bring to the boil. Cook for 2 minutes more.
- Take off the heat and add the butter, the parsley and the crushed garlic.

Po

Torino

Asti

Airasca

Pinerolo   Carmagnola

● Torre Pellice

Restaurant **Flipot**
Corso Gramsci, 17
Torre Pellice, Torino

Spring Risotto with Fresh Herbs and Freshwater Prawns

Poverty sharpens inventiveness and in the past, wild herbs were picked and used to flavour simple dishes. These days, on the contrary, they have been "re-discovered" as refined and rare ingredients and most people are completely unfamiliar with wild edible plants. Delicate flavours predominate in this dish - that of fresh herbs and of river prawns, sweeter than sea prawns.

Ingredients

- 350 g Baldo rice
- 20 river prawns
- 1 bunch nettle tips
- 1 bunch watercress
- 1 bunch hop shoots
- 1 bunch wild cabbage
- 1 tablespoon extra virgin olive oil
- 1 shallot
- 1 knob of butter
- 1 litre poultry stock, very light, boiling
- salt

- Blanch all the herbs in salty boiling water (place them in the pot when the water boils and strain them off as soon as it boils again). Cool, dry and chop well.
- Place the freshwater prawns in boiling water and cook for 2-3 minutes. Cool and peel them.
- Lightly fry the chopped shallot in a pan with oil, then add the chopped herbs and the whole freshwater prawns.
- Sauté for 1-2 minutes, add the rice, fry for 1 minute, then add the boiling stock until covering the rice.
- Cook for 15 minutes stirring occasionally and adding a little stock each time, only when necessary.
- At the end of the cooking, remove from the heat, add the butter and blend: the risotto should be soft and creamy.
- Serve immediately decorating each dish with a prawn head.

Recommended wine

Alto Adige Terlano – Pinot bianco

Grapes *pinot bianco, others max. 10%*
Region *Trentino Alto Adige*

Restaurant **Al Sorriso**
Via Roma, 18
Soriso, Novara

106

Risotto with Cartizze Wine and Red Treviso Chicory

Are you sure you can pick out red Treviso chicory among others varieties? If you intend to prepare this dish you must do so. Actually, their impressive appearance - bright red long fine leaves with a crisp white central part - make them easily identifiable. It is certainly the most appreciated variety of chicory, unique for its sweet-sour taste which is carried over to the rice, in particular when combining its flavour with Cartizze wine and Parmigiano Reggiano cheese.

Ingredients

- 350 g Arborio rice
- 200 g Treviso chicory hearts
  (and a few more for decorating)
- 100 g butter
- 1 small onion, finely chopped
- 50-80 g grated Parmesan
- 2 litres boiling stock
- 4 dl good Cartizze wine
- salt and freshly ground black pepper

- Wash the chicory hearts well and cut them into four to six lenghts.
- Lightly fry the onion in a pan with 50 g butter on moderate heat, when it starts to brown, add the chicory hearts and the rice and sauté for 1 minute. Add the wine and allow it to evaporate a little.
- Add a ladleful of hot stock and stir. When the rice has absorbed almost all the stock, add another ladleful and continue in this way, a ladleful at a time, until the end of the cooking, stirring occasionally to prevent the rice from sticking to the bottom.
- When the rice is cooked, remove from the heat, add the remaining butter and the Parmesan and blend.
- Taste for salt, add freshly-ground black pepper to choice and serve on heated dishes decorated with chicory hearts.

Recommended wine

Prosecco di Conegliano Valdobbiadene superiore di Cartizze secco

Grapes *pinot bianco, pinot grigio*
Region *Veneto*

Restaurant **Le tre panoce**
Via Vecchia Trevigiana, 50
Conegliano, Treviso

Risotto with Lobster and Lard

*I*n this recipe lobster is combined with Colonnata pork lard... A meeting between sea and land, of two different kinds of sweetness. Colonnata lard is a delicate and traditional product that dates back to the early Carrara marble miners. And as in all self-respecting marriages... rice must be thrown.

Ingredients

- 300 g Vialone Nano rice
- 2 lobsters
- 1,5 litres of court-bouillon
- 4 basil leaves
- 4 rosemary leaves
- 50 g pancetta
- 1 spring onion
- 8 thin slices Siena bacon
- 20 g whipped lard
- extra virgin olive oil for dressing
- 50 g grated Parmesan
- salt and black pepper

- Remove the pincers from the lobsters and cook them for 8 minutes in the court-bouillon.
- Cut the lobsters in half length-wise, season with salt, pepper, olive oil, basil and rosemary. Leave for 15 minutes to absorb flavours.
- Place the pancetta (in very fine slices) and the finely chopped onion in a pan. Leave over a moderate heat until soft (do not fry). When the onion is tender but not brown, add the rice and leave to take flavour.
- Add the court-bouillon, a ladleful at a time, and only after the previous one has been absorbed.
- While the rice is cooking, put the lobsters in the oven at 150° for 4-5 minutes (depending on their size). Remove their juice and wrap them in the slices of pancetta.
- By now the rice will be *al dente*. Remove from the heat, add the whipped lard and the Parmesan and blend, mixing in the pieces of cooked lobster meat.
- Place the lobster wrapped in the pancetta in the oven at 150° for 30 seconds.
- Put the risotto on the dishes and decorate with the lobster. Sprinkle with black pepper and a little raw olive oil.

Recommended wine

Trentino Traminer Aromatico

Grapes *traminer aromatico*
Region *Trentino Alto Adige*

Rest. **Gambero Rosso**
Piazza della Vittoria, 72
San Vincenzo, Livorno

Risotto with Brown Fennel

e have lost the greater part - if not all - of our culinary knowledge on aromatic herbs. In the past, wild herbs, mainly in springtime, provided a different touch to each dish. Very few are used these days and these are always the same: parsley, fennel, marjoram, thyme, sage... And very often they are not even fresh. Welcome then, a risotto that is a surprise for its very simplicity. It may not be easy to find brown fennel, but that is exactly what is needed, because its taste and aroma are delicate and less intense than better-known wild green fennel.

Ingredients

- 280 g Carnaroli rice
- 3 dl veal and hen stock
- 3 knobs of butter
- 1 bunch small brown fennel sprigs
- 6 tablespoons freshly grated Parmesan

Recommended wine

(Albana di Romagna secco)

Grapes *albana*
Region *Emilia Romagna*

- Bring the stock to the boil in a pan, add the rice and the butter. Bring to boil on low heat stirring with a wooden spoon.
- Halfway through cooking (after approx. 7 minutes), take half the fennel sprigs and cut them with scissors directly over the rice in the pan. The herbs must be picked the same morning as cooking and kept, unwashed, in a closed glass jar until using them.
- When the rice is almost ready (neither too dry nor too liquid), remove from the heat and stir while adding the grated Parmesan.
- Leave to rest for 2-3 minutes. Sprinkle the rest of the fennel (scissors cut) over the rice and serve.

Restaurant **Lancellotti**
Via Grandi, 120
Soliera, Modena

Risotto with Pumpkin Flowers and Truffles

the term "pumpkin flowers" refers to the male and female flowers of pumpkins and courgettes. When buying them, the flowers must be glossy, closed and present a fine yellow-orange colour at the edges. They must be consumed the same day.

Although cookbooks rarely mention the fact, pumpkin flowers were used in different ways in peasant cooking, to accompany fries and themselves fried in oil (often stuffed). But in the last ten years pumpkin or marrow flowers, as so many "poor" ingredients, have become popular and can now be found in the market all the year round.

Ingredients

- 300 g Carnaroli rice
- 50 g butter
- 1 finely chopped garlic clove
- 50 g approx. pumpkin flowers
- 1 litre boiling veal stock
- 2 tablespoons extra virgin olive oil
- half a tablespoon finely chopped onion
- 0,5 dl dry white wine
- 1 tablespoon grated Parmesan
- 1 white truffle (approx. 60 g)
- sea salt

- Separate the petals of the pumpkin flowers from the stalk and the calyx: wash and dry them well and cut them into 3-4 pieces.
- Sauté the garlic in a frying pan with 35 g of butter, add the flowers and leave them for a minute to take flavour. Then gradually add a little stock at a time until the end of the cooking (about 15 minutes), taste for salt and remove them from the pan.
- In a pot sauté the chopped onion in the olive oil and 15 g of butter; add the rice and sauté for 2 minutes on a very low heat.
- Add the wine and allow it to evaporate. Add a ladleful of stock, stir and continue the cooking adding a ladleful at a time as soon as the rice is dry.
- After 10-12 minutes (3/4 of cooking time), add the pumpkin flowers, stir well and continue cooking.
- Two minutes before the end of cooking time, add the Parmesan, taste for salt and blend.
- Take the risotto off the fire when it is al dente and serve immediately on heated plates garnished with the freshly cut truffle slices.

Recommended wine

> **Alto Adige Pinot nero riserva**

Grapes *Pinot nero 95%, others red max. 5%*
Region *Alto Adige*

> *Restaurant* **Aimo e Nadia**
> Via Montecuccoli, 6
> Milan

Sardinian Risotto

According to Sardinian tradition, when the pig was slaughtered the meat was "preserved" in aromatic herbs to give it flavour. The herbs were different in each area; some used mountain thyme, others fennel and others simply garlic. The aromatised meat was left to rest for a day and then used to prepare this "November" rice.

Ingredients

- 250 g Sant'Andrea rice
- 5 tablespoons extra virgin olive oil
- 1 garlic clove
- half a white onion
- 125 g herbal pork meat or semi-dry seasoned sausage
- 1,5 dl young Vernaccia wine
- 2 Camona tomatoes
- 0,75 liters of stock made with the pork bones
- 0,15 g saffron powder
- 50 g grated sheep cheese
- grated lemon skin
- salt

- Lightly fry the whole crushed garlic clove and the finely sliced onion in the oil. When the onion is brown and has flavoured the oil, remove it.
- Add the meat or sausage (hand-broken in pieces) and leave to dissolve in the pan for 5 minutes while stirring; add the Vernaccia and leave to evaporate on intense heat.
- Add the peeled and chopped tomatoes; leave in the pan for about 7 minutes until they take on the flavours. (Camona are a Sardinian variety of firm and sweetish tomatoes).
- Add the stock, taste for salt and bring to the boil.
- After half an hour, add the saffron and then the rice. Cover and cook on low heat for 15 minutes without stirring.
- Remove from the heat. Add the goat's cheese and a generous helping of grated lemon peel; Blend gently and serve.

Recommended wine

(Carignano del Sulcis rosso)

Grapes *carigenano, others15%*
Region *Sardinia*

Restaurant of the **Hotel Gallura**
Corso Umberto, 145
Olbia, Sassari

Risotto with Saffron Threads and Chicken Oyster in Red Wine

t he secret of this dish lies precisely in the chicken, which must be top-quality and farm bred; in other words, hard to find these days. The rice absorbs its flavour and is crowned by its most exquisite part, its "oyster" or *sot-l'y-laisse*, as the French call it, meaning so delicious that it cannot be left for others…And the author of the recipe describes the dish, when prepared for just a couple, as an "egoism for two", because to obtain the two oysters a whole chicken must be sacrificed.

Ingredients

- 350 g Carnaroli rice
- 2 chicken carcasses
- 120 g butter
- 4 dl full-bodied red wine
- 10 g dry porcini mushrooms, softened in warm water
- half a celery stalk
- half a carrot
- 1 onion
- 1 g saffron threads
- 2 litres boiling meat stock
- 30 gr grated Parmesan
- salt and freshly ground black pepper

Recommended wine

Barbera d'Alba

Grapes *barbera*
Region *Piedmont*

Restaurant **Pierino**
via XXIV Maggio 36
Viganò Brianza, Como

- Lightly fry the chicken carcasses in a pot (i.e. without heads, drumsticks, viscera and breasts) in 10 g butter. Add half the onion, the celery, the carrot and the mushrooms (chopped and softened in water) until obtaining a good cooking base.
- Add the wine, leave to evaporate, reduce the heat, add the meat stock and cook gently for 20 minutes. Taste for salt and pepper. At the end of the cooking, remove the oysters from the chicken with a small spoon: this is the most delicious part of the bird and is situated where the drumsticks are joined to the hip.
- Off the heat, whip the sauce adding 40 g of cold butter.
- In a large pot lightly fry a tablespoon of the chopped onion in 20 g butter, then add the rice and sauté it for a minute on moderate heat
- Add a ladleful of hot stock and stir. When the rice has absorbed almost all the stock, add another ladleful. Continue in this way, a ladleful at a time, until the rice is cooked.
- Two minutes before the end, add the saffron threads previously dissolved in 6 tablespoons of stock.
- Turn off the heat, add the remaining butter and the grated Parmesan and blend. Taste for salt. Serve the risotto on warmed dished with the chicken oysters in the centre covered with the red wine sauce.

Risotto with Riviera Artichokes

he Romans adored artichokes and Plinius was indignant: "Is this how we convert monstrosities of the land into a festive meal - products even the animals instinctively avoid?" he says in Book XX of his *Naturalis Historia*. In spite of all his wisdom, Plinius ignored that the monstrosity was a flower, with thorns, true, but even so a flower. And what does a flower transmit? A sensation of delicacy. So let us forget the thorns and enjoy the exquisitely sweet flavour the artichoke gives to this risotto.

Ingredients

- 350 g Carnaroli rice
- 5 Riviera artichokes
- 2 litres chicken carcass stock (see p. 118)
- 4 tablespoons extra virgin olive oil
- 1 tablespoon chopped shallot
- 60 g very fresh butter
- 70 g grated Parmesan (if possible old so it melts easily without forming threads)

- 2 dl dry white Soave wine
- 2 blanched garlic cloves
- parsley leaves
- 1 de-salted well washed anchovy fillet
- 2 tablespoon black truffle "juice" (bought prepared)
- Parmesan cheese, finely sliced
- juice of 1 lemon
- freshly ground white and black pepper

Recommended wine

(Franciacorta rosso)

Grapes *cabernet franc 40-50%, barbera 20-30%, nebbiolo 15-25%, merlot 10-15%; athers, max. 10%*

Region *Lombardy*

Antica Osteria del Ponte
Cassinetta
di Lugagnano, Milan

- Clean the artichokes by cutting off the stalks and removing the hard outer leaves. Place the tender inner part in a pot with cold water and lemon juice. Wash the stalks and outer leaves and slowly bring to the boil in the stock.
- Place the minced shallot in a frying pan with 40 g butter and 2 tablespoons of olive oil. While the shallot is frying lightly (without browning), cut the artichokes in quarters, remove the inner threads and slice finely. Add the shallot and cook for 30 seconds to take flavour.
- Add the rice and sauté it for 2 minutes stirring with a wooden spoon.
- Add the wine and let it evaporate completely. Then add a ladleful of previously strained boiling stock, blend and continue cooking, adding a ladleful of stock as soon as the previous one is almost completely absorbed.
- While the rice is cooking, prepare the sauce to be added at the end of the cooking. In a medium-sized pan put a soupspoonful of olive oil, the blanched garlic cloves (boiled twice in salty water), the anchovy and the parsley sprigs. Leave to take flavour then add a ladleful of stock. Reduce the stock to half and add the black truffle juice. Blend with a tablespoon of olive oil and another of grated Parmesan in an electric blender.
- When the rice is almost cooked, remove from the heat, let rest for 3 to 4 minutes, then add a tablespoon of olive oil, the butter and the remaining Parmesan.
- Serve on hot plates with a little sauce in the centre. Sprinkle to taste with the slices of Parmesan and plenty of pepper and serve immediately.

Creamy Rice with Broad Beans and Morels

Morels (*Morchella*) are strangely-shaped mushrooms whose caps look like upside-down pineapples completely pitted with irregular holes. They appear in spring in several varieties, varying in colour from ochre to dark brown and blackish. Even the white tasty stalk of the morel is used. In traditional cuisine it is cooked in cream and served as garnish for small game dishes. In traditional Italian cooking, the morel is a common ingredient in Emilia, where it is served with fresh pasta. The "veal juice" mentioned in the recipe is prepared with veal rumen cut in small pieces. Brown it over a strong heat and then remove its fat by boiling it for half an hour. This stock is then strained, reduced to three quarters and blended with a tablespoon of olive oil.

Ingredients

For the morels

- 100 g well washed morels
- 1 tablespoon minced onion
- 2 tablespoons carrots cut in dices
- 20 g butter
- 1 dl veal juice
- juice of half a lemon
- salt

For the rice

- 320 g Carnaroli rice
- 1 tablespoon chopped shallot
- 1-2 litres boiling chicken stock
- 1 dl dry white wine
- 40 g salted butter
- 50 g grated Grana cheese
- 2 tablespoons white wine vinegar
- 10 g flakes Grana cheese
- 100 g podded broad beans
- freshly grated black pepper

- Lightly fry the onion with the carrot and butter in a pan. Add the lemon juice and let evaporate. Then add the whole morels, the veal juice and cook for 10 minutes on a low heat and with the pan covered.
- Then prepare the risotto: sauté the shallot in 20 g butter, add the rice and fry. Add the white wine and leave to evaporate completely.
- Add the boiling stock a little at a time and only when the previous addition is almost completely absorbed, until the end of cooking.
- When the rice is *al dente*, remove from the heat and add the white wine vinegar, the remaining butter, the Grana cheese and the pepper. Serve in deep dishes with the morels and the beans (kept in water and ice until using them) and the Grana cheese flakes.

Recommended wine

> **Sangiovese di Romagna riserva**
>
> **Grapes** *sangiovese, min. 85%; others red,, max. 15%*
> **Region** *Emilia Romagna*

> *Restaurant* **Da Giannino**
> Via Sciesa, 8
> Milan

Spring Risotto

t his dish (*Risotto Primavera*) is a classic at Harry's Bar in Venice, appearing on their menu for the last thirty years. It is also known as Torcello-style risotto, in honour of the delicious vegetables that grow on the island of the same name and which make this dish so unique. The ingredients may very according to the season. Thus we have artichokes and asparagus in spring, marrows in summer and mushrooms in autumn. As these days it is fairly easy to find vegetables in the market at all seasons, they can be used all at the same time, only avoiding eggplant, which would ruin its colour.

Ingredients For the vegetables

- 5 tablespoons extra virgin olive oil
- 1 garlic clove, crushed
- 225 g mushroom caps
- 6 small (or 1 large) artichokes
- 2 small tablespoons finely chopped onion
- 4 small courgettes
- 12 asparagus
- half a red pepper
- 1 tomato
- white part of a medium sized leek
- salt and freshly ground black pepper

For the risotto

- 250 g Carnaroli or Vialone Nano rice
- 1 tablespoons extra virgin olive oil
- 1 small onion, chopped
- 1,5 litres boiling chicken stock
- 45 g butter at room temperature
- 80 g grated Parmesan,
plus a little more to serve at the table
- salt and freshly ground black pepper

- Start with the vegetables: on medium heat, heat the oil in a large pan, add the garlic, sauté for 30 seconds and remove.
- Add the finely sliced mushrooms and cook for 5-6 minutes until tender and the liquid released has evaporated. Add the finely sliced artichoke hearts and cook for 8-10 minutes, until tender. Add the onion and cook for 2 minutes more.

- Add all at the same time the courgettes, the asparagus, the red pepper, the tomato and the leek, all cut in small pieces (2-3 cm). Turn up the heat and cook for 10 minutes, stirring frequently until all the vegetables are cooked, tasting for salt and pepper (You can also cook each vegetable separately).
- To prepare the rice, heat the oil in a pan, add the onion and fry lightly. When it starts to brown, add the rice stirring for 1 minute.
- Add a ladleful of boiling stock and stir. As soon as the stock is absorbed, add another ladleful. Continue in this way until the end of cooking.
- After 10 minutes add half the prepared vegetables.
- At the end of cooking, remove the risotto from the heat (the grains should be loose and *al dente*), add the butter and the Parmesan and blend. Taste for salt and pepper. Keep stirring and add two or three tablespoons of stock for a deliciously smooth risotto.
- Serve immediately with grated Parmesan in a separate dish.

Recommended wine

(Soave)

Grapes *garganega, min. 70%, and/or pinot bianco, chardonnay and trebbiano di Soave, max. 30%*

Region *Veneto*

Restaurant **Harry's Bar**
Calle Vallaresso, 1323
Venice

Rice Sartù with Eggplant

his recipe reveals the products and the fantasy typical of Naples. The dish is not strictly a risotto, but starts as risotto and ends as a *sartù*, a sublime dish and source of continual surprise.

Ingredients *For the sartù*

- 300 g rice
- 150 g peas
- 100 g extra virgin olive oil
- 1 onion
- 1 dl white wine
- 1,5 litres hot chicken stock
- 150 g lean veal meat, minced
- soft breadcrumbs (from 1 small loaf, soaked in milk)
- 3 egg yolks
- nutmeg
- 2 chicken livers
- 2 tablespoons brandy
- 150 g of mozzarella
- 1 tablespoon breadcrumbs
- 1 tablespoon grated Parmesan
- 2 eggplants
- salt and black pepper

For the tomato cream

- 40 g extra virgin olive oil
- half an onion
- 60 g carrot
- 60 g celery
- 80 g minced veal meat
- 1 dl white wine
- 6 dl San Marzano tomato puré
- 1 bay leaf

- Prepare the tomato cream: finely chop the onion, carrot and celery and lightly fry in the oil. Add the meat, stir, add the white wine and allow it to evaporate. Add the tomato puré and the bay leaf.
- Cook on low heat for about 30 minutes. Then remove the bay leaf and pass through the potato mincer.
- Prepare the rice *sartù*: make a risotto using olive oil, a whole onion, the peas (boiled once), the white wine and the chicken stock.
- Remove the risotto from the heat three quarter ways through cooking time. Remove the whole onion and spread the rice on a marble surface to detain the cooking process.

- Place the minced meat, the milk-soaked breadcrumbs, one egg yolk, salt, pepper and a little nutmeg in a pan. Stir and blend all the ingredients. Form meatballs the size of an almond, flour and fry them in oil.
- Sauté the chicken livers in a pan with the brandy (after removing their skin and bile sac).
- In another pot, blend the risotto with two egg yolks, the mozzarella cut in dice, the livers, the parmesan and the meat balls.
- Cut the eggplant in fine slices and fry them in the olive oil.
- Grease a 20 cm diameter oven mould with oil; sprinkle with breadcrumbs then line with the fried eggplant. Fill with the risotto and cook in the oven at 180° for 15 minutes.
- Remove from the oven, de-mould and serve on the tomato cream.

Recommended wine

(Isola di Ischia Piedirosso)

Grapes *piedirosso (Per' e Palumbo)*
Region *Campania*

Restaurant **Don Alfonso 1890**
Piazza Sant'Agata, 11
Sant'Agata sui due Golfi NA

Creamy Risotto with Hop Shoots and Milky Cod Stew

n this dish an unusual meeting between two different flavours takes place: that of *bruscanzoli*, spring hop shoots, and cod, dry and soaked and sweetened when cooked in milk. The result is something unique, both delicate and intense.

Ingredients *For the risotto*

- 300 g Vialone Nano rice
- 150 g (bruscanzoli) green tender hop shoots
- 5 dl boiling meat stock
- 100 g butter
- 80 g grated Parmesan
- 8 cl extra virgin olive oil
- 2 shallots
- 2 garlic cloves

For the cod stew

- 200 g soaked dry cod
- 5 and a half tablespoons extra virgin olive oil
- 1 garlic clove
- 1 onion
- 1 bay leaf
- 5 dl milk

- To prepare the cod stew, put a pan on the heat with 1 l water. When it boils add the cod (previously soaked during 24 hours) and when it starts boiling again remove the fish and skin it.
- Put 2 and a half tablespoons of oil, the chopped onion and a whole garlic clove (take this out halfway through cooking) in a pan and lightly fry on moderate heat until it is a golden colour.
- Add the cod, fry it for a moment then add the cold milk. Add the bay leaf and cook for at least 20 minutes on very low heat.
- In the meantime put the oil, the chopped onion, a whole garlic (take this out halfway through cooking) and when they are golden, add the clean washed hops and braise for 10 minutes covering it all with half a ladleful of boiling stock.
- To prepare the risotto, sauté the rice alone in a pot on high heat for 4 minutes stirring carefully, making sure it does not burn.
- Add a ladleful of stock and stir. When almost all the stock is absorbed add another ladleful. Continue in this way until the end of cooking.
- When the rice is *al dente*, add the braised hops, remove from the heat, add the butter, a tablespoon of olive oil and the grated parmesan and blend.
- Serve *all'onda* with the stew on top of the risotto.

Recommended wine

(Lugana)

Grapes *trebbiano di Lugana, others white max. 10%*
Region *Veneto*

Restaurant **Perbellini**
Via Muselle, 10/11
Isola Rizza, Verona

The Future of Rice

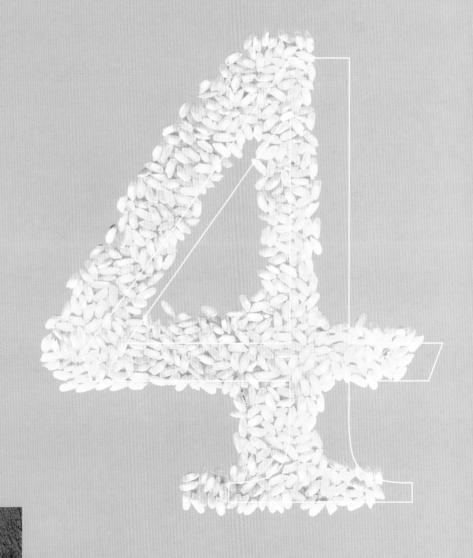

The future of rice

The end of the millennium will be long remembered by the rice producers of the Piemonte, Lombardy, Veneto and other Italian areas (Emilia Romagna, Sardinia and Calabria) where this crop plays a major role in the country's agricultural economy. This will not be nostalgia for the past, Fellini's Amarcord-style, but, to refer to another famous film, rather a "*bitter memory*" because, compared to the situation at the beginning of the nineties, the year 2000 opens with serious problems in the sector.

A change with many consequences

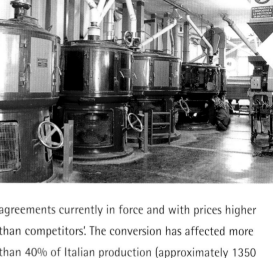

Prices have fallen as a result of the elimination of protective barriers in the European Union, but also of the arrival on the European markets of rice produced in the United States (in particular in Bill Clinton's state of Arkansas), Thailand and other Far East countries: long-grain rice of the *indica* subspecies, mostly used as garnish, in salads and fast foods. Italian rice-growers, seduced by the mermaids' call of mass consumption, have attempted to produce these varieties in Italy instead of the traditional ones, of the *japonica* subspecies. Their efforts have not been very successful, hindered by international trade agreements currently in force and with prices higher than competitors'. The conversion has affected more than 40% of Italian production (approximately 1350 million kilos) and have placed rice-growing in Italy in a critical situation.

Perhaps there was no other solution. The market would probably not have been able to absorb such large quantities of rice used mostly for dishes requiring "lengthy cooking and an elaborate preparation". Today consumers not only demand risottos, rice bombs and sartùs. They also - and mainly - demand fast food and pre-cooked dishes to heat at home, as well as exotic and multiethnic dishes. The current market is as a result one open to those varieties of rice that allow fast cooking and which do not overcook, such as parboiled and perfumed rice like Basmati and Patna.

These tendencies, at the time duly announced by the market gurus - always belied by reality but never

This page, left: Scotti industrial rice production plant. The rice is transported through ducts from below to above (from the hulling machines on the first floor to the blanching and glazing operations on the upper floors).

Right: Scotti rice sifters.

Previous page, top: Scotti rice hulling industrial machines.

Left: Packets of oriental rice.

contradicted by the media, confirmed moreover by many in the marketing world seduced by the mirage instead of being attentive to real data - have "pushed" Italian rice production up against unfavourable and certainly unexpected international decisions (specific agreements, customs barriers, etc.).

The producers themselves have perhaps not reacted with sufficient confidence in the popularity of Italian cooking in the world, which could be used to reinforce and to promote quality rice suitable for risottos and other gourmet dishes in its conquest of foreign markets.

Positive efforts

In spite of everything, the future should not be seen through the pessimism of reason, but through the optimism of resolution, precisely because Italy has the most interesting heritage of top quality rice, varieties preferred by haute cuisine both "public" (restaurants)

and "private" (quality home cooking). At this level, Italian rice is the unquestionable star, used for risottos, minestre fisse, timbales, sartùs and not just a secondary ingredient used for salads, side dishes and similar preparations.

But to become a leader on the international scene, Italian rice, taking advantage of the current popularity of Italian cuisine - including extraordinary risottos specialities (with meat, fish, vegetable, cheese, sausages, etc.) - requires an even more intense reassessment. One of the problems is that in other countries, even in those where Italian cooking enjoys a healthy popularity, the organoleptic differences and the cooking techniques of the different varieties of rice produced in the Piemonte, Lombardy, Veneto, Emilia Romagna and Sardinia are unknown. Undoubtedly it is necessary to export a risotto culture, but it is also essential to promote information on all the different varieties, together with their specific features, of this millennial cereal.

Rice and wine

The situation of Italian rice today could be compared to that of Italian wine in the sixties, when the world

started appreciating Italian production but in general ignored the differences between the one wine and another. So what other features of interest should be taken into account in a revaluation of Italian rice, apart from a superficial promotion of the art of the risotto in restaurants, cooking schools and homes?

A specific data is that some varieties of rice - those appropriate for risottos, such as Carnaroli, Arborio, Vialone nano, Baldo or Roma - grow better in specific areas, either due to the microclimate, or to the terrain, or to a mysterious but real combination of several factors. This is confirmed by concrete examples, as in the case of Vialone nano which grows better in some Veronese areas than in others. Therefore, in a discussion on relative quality, the variety is immediately associated with the idea of a specific location, a combination that leads us directly to the concept of cru used for wine.

A rice for each risotto

However, all the above is not sufficient. More must be said. Italian rice must also rediscover - as already occurred in the eighties with the prince of rice, the Carnaroli - varieties that have disappeared or are disappearing, like the giant Vercelli, Maratelli, Razza 77 and so many others.

Each *haute cuisine* or *prêt-à-manger* dish based on a risotto should use, depending on the ingredients, a specific type of rice.

It is not a question of vain dreams or unrealistic optimism, but of results within possible reach. All that needed be done is to "culturally" spread and promote this extraordinary cereal - many varieties of which are grown exclusively in Italy - in those foreign markets in which Italian cooking is currently emerging.

Carnaroli rice and preparations for Arborio and Carnaroli risottos and rice soups.

134

Restaurants
and Index

Notes on restaurants

AIMO E NADIA page 114

Aimo Moroni and his wife Nadia are among the very few Tuscan restaurateurs living in Milan who offer *made in Italy*-style quality cuisine.

Cooking there is simple, light and genuine, with well-defined tastes and flavours, enhanced by top-quality ingredients that Aimo chooses very carefully and his wife Nadia prepares in the kitchen in perfect combinations. Wide range of proposals: veal leg in bean salad; raw tomato soup with olive oil, basil and *crostini*; spaghetti with onion and chilli; eggplant stuffed with fresh cheese and aromatic herbs; *sanato* entrecote; rabbit with bay and fresh pistachios; kidneys with cauliflower; pumpkin flowers with *ricotta* (sheep's cheese) and mushrooms. Fascinating trolley loaded with cheeses (all hand made) and sweets (*bacio* with hazelnuts and chocolate, chestnut flour crepes with ricotta and acacia honey, fresh fruit sherbets).

via Montecuccoli, 6 • Milan • tel. 02 416886

AL SORRISO page 106

Al Sorriso, a genuine pearl of a quality restaurant, offers the pleasant view of a delightful village on the banks of Lake Orta, the comfort of a small hotel and a dining-room for only twenty-five guests. In the kitchen, the expert cook Luisa Valazza and in the dining-room, her husband Angelo, who is also in charge of the wine list.

In addition to a couple of tasty menus (made up of four courses plus a rich selection of local cheeses, desserts and sweets) there is a long list of "specials" to order from: *capesante* stew with cannellini beans and lard with chives; yellow pumpkin and ginger cream with Sanremo prawns; borlotti bean cream with prawns and Formazza Valley *pancetta* with basil; *filoni* with truffles and medallions of piedmontese *fassone* stuffed with *foie gras*; *fagottini* rabbit with rosemary; roast baby pigeons with Modena balsamic vinegar. Desserts include cedar flavoured mint sherbets, banana and honey custard or *gianduia* cake with cold syllabub.

Via Roma, 18 • Soriso, Novara • tel. 0322 983228

ANTICA OSTERIA DEL PONTE page 120

Ezio Santin - proprietor of the Antica Osteria del Ponte, an old fifteenth-century Trattoria converted into an exquisite restaurant - carries the love of good cuisine in his blood. He puts real feeling into his celebrated dishes based on French cuisine with Italian products and flavour.

They include his remarkable lobster ravioli with marrow sauce, eggs wrapped in foie gras sauce and white truffles, lamb saddle with aromatic herbs, smoked eggplants and marrow with tomato sauce, Riviera fish fillets with aromatic oil; rabbit fillets with eggplant *caponatina*.

Desserts (prepared by their son Maurizio) include millefeuille with *gianduia* or coffee cream, chocolate mousse with almonds and hazelnuts and caramel honey cake with sherbet.

P.zza Negri, 9 • Cassinetta di Lugagnano MI • tel. 02 9420034

CASCINA BOVILE page 84

The Marianis, Pier Luigi in the kitchen and Roberta in the dining room (she is a sommelier and personally in charge of the winecellar), have converted an old country house into a spacious and comfortable restaurant.

The cooking is traditional and based on local products, mainly rice and goose. In fact, goose is the star here: in the mixed starters (cured, smoked or herbal goose breasts; cooked and raw goose salami; goose pâté, crackling goose skin and steamed goose terrina with mushrooms), followed by the risotti (with goose, with *fagiolini dall'occhio*, pork salami paste), with gnocchi and smoked goose breast, with goose-stuffed ravioli, roast goose and goose breast with tarragon.

Desserts (all home-made) include sherbets (of citrus fruits and green apples), pear charlotte, wild fruit Bavaroise, fruit crostate with cold muscatel syllabub, tiramisu and trifle.

In the cellar, the best Oltrepò Pavese, as well as other great regional, wines and a rare collection of grappas and whiskies.

Via Bovile, 2 • Ceretto Lomellina, Pavia • tel. 0384 56123

COCCHI page 96

Parma is well known for its excellent cuisine but Cocchi, owned by Corrado Cocchi, is one of the few family restaurants that serve traditional local and regional dishes in the galliot line.

The meal can start with a generous helping of raw ham, *culatello* and double salami (fresh or cured, according to taste) and continue with one of many possible delights prepared by the talented Laura Cocchi.

Oven-cooked rice bomb (speciality of the house), *anolini* (with or without broth), *garganelli* with duck sauce, potato *tortelli* with truffles.

Second course could be artichoke-stuffed veal, lamb with aromatic herbs, parmesan-flavoured tripe or a splendid *carrello di bollito*. And for dessert a melon Bavaroise, *semifreddo croccante* or a syllabub charlotte. Ample supply of wines selected by the son of the owner, Daniele.

Via Gramsci, 16 • Parma • tel. 0521 981990

DA BALIN page 100

"Panissa with Boldo rice, risotto Carnaroli with artichokes and black truffles, risotto with chicory, marrow and saffron..." are the first dishes on the menu of Da Balin, a restaurant with a friendly rural atmosphere. Angelo Silvestro - with his wife Anna, cook and sommelier, at his side - is a true ambassador of Vercelli risotto in the world: every year he spends several weeks in Oregon (USA) teaching the art of this dish. Balin's dishes are deeply rooted in the genuine local cuisine (*bagna cauda*, *agnolotti* with roast sauce, *sottofiletto* of *fassone* with Barbera wine, goose with wild cabbage) as well as based on research into local products, like the cheeses served with *cugnà*. Unique are the gnocchi made with rice flour and served with pork lard.

Fraz. Castell'Apertole • Livorno Ferraris VC • tel. 0161 47121

DA GIANNINO page 122

This historical establishment - founded in 1899 as a Tuscan wineshop by Giannino Brindi - is today one of the most relevant restaurants in Milan. It consists of a series of charmingly decorated large and small dining-rooms and a magnificent winter garden. In the kitchen, Davide Oldani, a young but talented cook, prepares dishes based on fantasy and lightness: grilled *capesante* and white truffle salad; vegetable pâté in olive sauce, raw basil and leaks; *strichetti* with squid and chives; crisp gilthead fillet with cuscus; cuttlefish and pancetta in dried-bean sauce; *semifreddo* with walnuts, rum and persimmon compote; red wine jelly with strawberries and black pepper.

Via Sciesa, 8 • Milan • tel. 02 55195582 / 55195025

DA GUIDO page 86

Genuine temple of good national cuisine, Da Guido is named after the head of the family, Guido Alciati, who runs the business with his wife, sons and daughters-in-law. Cooking is based on the oldest traditional regional methods, updated and lightened in a unique and at times extraordinary way.

One of their secrets is research into the local products (from the goat kids of Murazzano to the *tome* and *robiole* of Castelmagno and Roccaverano). Specialities include tuna-filled baked peppers, risotto with sausage and pumpkin flowers, turkey hen fillets marinated with olives, baked duck with saffron sauce and red wine, *torrone* and sweets.

P.zza Umberto I, 27 • Costigliole d'Asti, Asti • tel. 0141 966012

DALL'AMELIA page 90

Discerning wine connoisseur, Dino Boscarato is a model of restaurant owner-manager, one of the few in able to run an establishment like the Trattoria dell'Amelia with more than two hundred place settings while maintaining the highest level in the kitchen (with a brigade of ten cooks commanded by chef Gianpietro Pes) and in the dining rooms (with Daniel Nicoletti in charge of the service, which is exquisite). Several set-price menus are available, mainly fish-based (always fresh) prepared according to either typical regional recipes or to creative inventions.

The restaurant has two special areas, one exclusively dedicated to fried or grilled fish, and the other to crustaceans, molluscs and Venetian *stuzzichini*. Desserts include excellent ice creams and pastries.

Via Miranese, 113 • Mestre, Venice • tel. 041 913951

DAL PESCATORE page 102

Antonio Santini, the perfect host in the dining room, and his wife Nadia, reigning in the kitchen, have transformed Dal Pescatore, the old family trattoria, into one of Italy's "top" restaurants. Not-to-be-missed starters include traditional antipasti (*culatello*, Mantua salami, *ciccioli*), *gras pistá* (pressed lard), tomato compote, eggplants with Tuscan olive oil, porcini mushrooms and foie gras. First course could be *agnolini* in hen stock and Lambrusco, snail soup or pumpkin *tortelli*.

"Specials" include horse stew with Barbera wine, baked veal hock with wild majoram; frogs' legs with herbs, sucking lamb saddle with Cabernet, duckling with balsamic vinegar or marinated orange-flavoured tench.

Grand finale with homemade desserts: *pipasener* and syllabub, chocolate pudding with vanilla cream, hot raspberry *crostata*, *cassata* with melted chocolate.

Strada Canneto Fontanella, 17 • Canneto sull'Oglio MN • Località Runate • tel. 0376 723001

DON ALFONSO 1890 page 126

Alfonso Iaccarino and his wife Livia have turned to Don Alfonso 1890 into a temple of "good eating", whose fame has already spread beyond national borders.

Elegant and cosy, the establishment includes a delightful terrace-garden with a splendid view of the gulfs of Naples and Sorrento. The dishes are original and refined, a combination of land and sea products: prawn-stuffed new onions; crayfish with egg in a jacket on a bed of French beans and beet; tripe with tomato, chilli, mussels and *cannellini*; velouté of fresh garlic with smoked eel and bread crusts, *tagliatelle* with meat sauce and chilli; mixed fry of baby squids and prawns, spinach and artichokes; *involtino* di *dentice* with *rucola* (rocket salad) and fennel root.

P.zza Sant'Agata, 11 • Sant'Agata sui due Golfi, Naples • tel. 081 8780026

FLIPOT page 104

Walter Eynard and his wife Gisella run the Flipot located in an eighteenth-century building. The restaurant is a both friendly and elegant place offering dishes that combine tradition and fantasy in a brilliant expression of professionality and passion. You can start the meal with eggplant and tomato aspic with watercress cream, *cocottina* with roast angler and foie gras, eel terreen with pepper sauce or wild cumin-flavoured pork ear salad.

As second course you could have a risotto with artichoke hearts and veal chine, chickpeas *tagliatelle* with asparagus and prawns, gnocchi gratin with sausages, onion and tomato, sucking pig carré cooked in *fieno de maggengo* or duck casserole.

As desserts their marron glacé Bavaroise, *sformato di fondente* in rosemary sauce, and nougat and hazelnut Genevoise are outstanding.

Corso Gramsci, 17 • Torre Pellice, Turin • tel. 0121 91236

GAMBERO ROSSO page 110

Fulvio Pierangeli - proprietor of the Gambero Rosso, an elegant restaurant looking over the small port of San Vincenzo - is an economist turned restaurateur for sheer love of cooking. A discerning connoisseur of both raw materials and cooking techniques, he combines land and sea ingredients in unusual and personal ways, as in his *passatina* of chickpeas with prawns, *frullato* of mussels with broccoli and caviar, fish raviolis with seafood sauce, gilthead fillet with red wine, millefeuille pistachio cream and fruit served with a small vanilla pudding.

Piazza Vittoria, 72 • S. Vincenzo, Livorno • tel. 0565 701021

HARRY'S BAR page 124

The attraction of Harry's Bar, a favourite jaunt of Hemingway and currently of the international jet-set and cultural world, is really unique. The proprietor, Arrigo Cipriani, is famous for his professionality and a strong defender of simple traditional Venetian dishes. As a result, his menu includes classics such as like *mantecato* codfish, tuna tartar, baby prawns with oil, pasta and string beans, lentil soup, *tagliolini* with cuttlefish, risotto with prawns and marrow, liver *alla veneziana*, prawns *alla Carlina*, baked gilthead fillets with tartar sauce, sautéd *Sanpietro* artichokes, Seabass fillets with capers.

Desserts are unbeatable, from the crepes with whipped cream to the cold chocolate mousse, from the sherbets to the ice creams. The wine list respects both tradition (with many Veneto wines) and distinction.

Calle Vallaresso, 1323 • Venecia • tel. 041 5285777

HOTEL GALLURA page 116

Rita Denza is the proprietress of the Hotel Gallura's restaurant, which offers excellent seafood dishes with fresh fish from both the Tyrrhenian and the Adriatic seas.

Her menu includes delicious Catalan salads, *tagliolini* with seaweeds and red mullet sauce, *linguine ai crostacei, fettuccine* with pumpkin flowers, *vermicelli* with clams in green sauce, *penne alla carbonara* with cuttlefish, *galluccio* Sassari style with garlic sauce and Cagliari-style with pine nuts and walnuts. Red mullet *sulla pietra* with fried sea anemone (known as *orciadas* here). The meat dishes are also excellent, in particular the sucking pig on a bed of myrtle and the sucking lamb, cooked in different ways. Desserts include puff pastry with fresh fruit and rum pudding. Wide selection of cheeses (goat's with herbs enriched with oil and smoked *ricotta*) and first-class wines, all Sardinian.

Corso Umberto, 145 • Olbia, Sassari • tel. 0789 24648

LANCELLOTTI page 112

The Lancellotti is run with enthusiasm, love and efficiency by all the members of the family: Emilio in charge of the dining-room with his brother Francesco (wines and balsamic vinegar), in the kitchen the third brother Angelo, the mother Ida and the "Boss", that is, the father who, as well as producing a good Lambrusco, selects the hams, *culatelli*, and salamis which they then cure at home.

Salads made with pears, raspberries, fresh herbs and balsamic vinegar, fresh homemade pastas seasoned with duck sauce, sausages, chives and sweet marjoram. Country soup with beans, baked veal liver stuffed with bacon and herbs.

Via Grandi, 120 • Soliera, Modena • tel. 059 567406

LE TRE PANOCE page 108

Armando Zanotto, *Armandino* to friends and proprietor of Le tre panoce, is considered the poet of red chicory, on which he has even written a recipe book, *Il radicchio in cucinar*. From September to March his restaurant, situated in an old seventeenth-century villa surrounded by fields, serves - together with a wide selection of Veneto specialities - starters, first courses, second courses, sauces, salads and even sweet desserts all based on chicory.

Via Vecchia Trevigiana, 50 • Conegliano TV • tel. 0438 60071

PERBELLINI page 128

Perbellini is an oasis of refined elegance half-hidden among the industrial buildings along the freeway that leads to Rovigo, about twenty kilometres from Verona. The proprietor, Giancarlo Perbellini (considered best chef of the new generations in 1997) is responsible for the imaginative cooking.

Starters, served on a glass tray include: seabass with chives, *sanpietro* with ginger curry, gilthead with celery, marinated prawns, red mullet fillets with honey, red beet and foie gras, seabass tartar with roast potatoes, stewed squid with asparagus and tomato. First courses include risotto *mantecato alla zuppa di pesce*, artichoke ravioli with prawns and fish soup.

Gilthead in leek crusts and bacon sauce is a delicious main dish. Also excellent pastries, strawberries sherbets and *strachin* millefeuille.

Via Muselle, 10/11 • Isola Rizza, Verona • tel. 045 7135352

PIERINO page 118

Pierino Penati's cuisine is based on a deep respect for tradition, both in the selection of the ingredients and in their use. Starters include a delicate rabbit ham salad; first course a risotto with leaks and potatoes or Gragnano spaghetti with clams *veraci* and red paprika. Fish dishes vary according to the season. Meat dishes include Milan-style cutlets, grilled veal with truffle sauce and polenta or kidneys with garlic and parsley.

The list of desserts include a delicious "experimental tart" based on ricotta and raw ham (*sic*), and with the coffee, some top-quality sweetmeats.

Via XXIV Maggio, 36 • Viganò Brianza, Como • tel. 039 956020

PILA VECIA page 92

Pila Vecia is not exactly a restaurant, but a dining-room for tasting risottos, located in the old warehouse of a seventeenth-century rice company. The current proprietor, Gabriele Ferron, has not only conserved the great paddle-wheel that drives the pounders used to shell the rice in mortars (*pile*) dug out of a single block of marble, but he has also created an "open kitchen" allowing all to see and understand the secrets of the preparation, processing and cooking of the dishes, all of course, based on rice. The menu varies according to the products available at the time.

But there is always a wide selection to chose, from risotto *Isola della Scala*-style to risottos with gorgonzola and spinach, cauliflower, pumpkin and asparagus market-garden-style, with green apples and oriental risotto (*ko samui*, with chicken breasts, peppers, onion, garlic and curry).

Via Saccovaner, 6 • Passolongo di Isola della Scala, Verona • tel. 045 7301022

PINOCCHIO page 98

Pinocchio is a temple to risotto that respects the traditions of a rice-growing land. It is run by its proprietor, Piero Bertinotti, with the help of his wife and daughters. The *paniscia alla novarese* is a historical dish not easy to find. The recipe used here is the classic one, but reinterpreted by Bertinotti, a rice enthusiast who prepares each item on the menu with utmost care. His wide offer of dishes include river prawn salad with cedar-flavoured *creste di gallo*, colt *costa* in *povr'om* sauce, snails in green butter and hazelnuts, and lemon-flavoured *Erika* cream.

Extraordinary selection of *alpeggio* and natural gorgonzola cheeses.

Via Matteotti, 147 • Borgomanero, Novara • tel. 0322 82273

PRATO GAIO page 88

Prato Gaio is a cosy typical Oltrepò-style trattoria run by the Liberti family who have been restaurateurs since the end of the nineteenth century. The cooking is traditional, regional and simple, but carried out with care and intelligence. A good example is the use of salty anchovy in a delicious and delicate sauce used with boiled meats, or hake with onion and raisins for the *raviolone*, or classic stuffing for capons and hens used here wrapped in lettuce and served with a delicious pepper *bagnetto*.

Via Versa, 16 • Montecalvo Versiggia, Pavia • tel. 0385 99726

ROMANO page 82

Romano is one of the best-known establishments of Versilia for its excellent seafood, in particular its mixed fries which *signora* Franca, wife of proprietor Romano Franceschini, prepares as light and digestible dishes. Starters include an excellent seabass fillet in *radicchio* sauce, hot seafood salad, prawns with bean purée, vegetable-stuffed squids and first-class crustaceans. Wide selection of remarkable first courses, all of them worthy of mention (but if the day's fishing was good, ask for spaghetti with clams, not included in the menu).

Second courses are a festival of flavours and freshness: baked turbot with potatoes and porcini mushrooms; baby octopus and prawns with marrow; grilled, baked or steamed *ombrine*. Desserts include an excellent creme brulée (a tribute paid by Franca and Romano to their friend Sirio Maccioni, of the Cirque of New York), rice and chocolate cake, fruit sherbets and pastry. The wine list comprises the best national and foreign names as well as several top-quality red wines.

Via Mazzini, 120 • Viareggio, Lucca • tel. 0584 31382

VIA VAI page 94

Skill and passion are the two nouns that best define Via Vai, owned by the Fagioli brothers (Stefano in the kitchen and Marco in the dining-room). Rich selection of cleverly up-dated traditional dishes of the Crema region: *zampone* with onion sauce, pumpkin *tortelli* with spices and candied fruit (rediscovery of a Venetian tradition transmitted by travellers from the lagoon), yellow risotto with pig tail sauce (a humble but tasty dish). Desserts include an excellent chocolate mousse with *mascarpone* cream. Ample wine list with a selection, in some cases personal, of quality crus - a wine cellar attended with loving care.

Via Libertà, 18 • Località Bolzone, Ripalta Cremasca, Cremona • tel. 0373 268232

index of risottos

index of wines